HOW CAN JAPANESE MANAGEMENT MAKE A POSITIVE CONTRIBUTION

Redesigning the Organization
for Productivity Improvement

Tomoko Makabe

The Edwin Mellen Press
Lewiston/Queenston/Lampeter

Library of Congress Cataloging-in-Publication Data

Makabe, Tomoko
    How can Japanese management make a positive contribution :
redesigning the organization for productivity improvement / Tomoko
Makabe.
        p.   cm.
    Includes bibliographical references (p.   ).
    ISBN 0-88946-159-7
    1. Electronic industries--Management--Case studies.
    2. Corporations, Japanese--Canada--Management--Case studies.
    3. Corporations, American--Canada--Management--Case studies.
    I. Title.
    HD9696.A2M36   1990
    621.381'068--dc20   89-13849
                                                                              CIP

ISBN 0-88946-159-7

A CIP catalog record for this book
is available from the British Library.

Copyright ©1991 The Edwin Mellen Press.

The Edwin Mellen Press   The Edwin Mellen Press
Box 450   Box 67
Lewiston, New York   Queenston, Ontario
USA 14092   CANADA L0S 1L0

The Edwin Mellen Press, Ltd.
Lampeter, Dyfed, Wales
UNITED KINGDOM SA48 7DY

Printed in the United States of America

For my late father,
Shunji Makabe

Contents

Acknowledgements

This book is about the sometimes rocky transition from American management to Japanese management within one television component manufacturing plant. The plant, situated in a small town in central Ontario, Canada, went through the transition process in the mid-1980's. I had the privilege of witnessing and documenting that process as an outsider-researcher.

I initiated this study as a continuation of my previous study on Japanese businesses in Canada while I was doing management studies as a Reorientation Fellow at the Faculty of Management Studies, University of Toronto. Pilot grants which allowed me to conduct a field survey were provided by Labour Canada's University Research Grants and the University of Toronto-York University Joint Centre on Modern Asia. I am indebted to the Faculty and the University for providing research facilities.

I would also like to express appreciation to the strategic research grant offered by the Social Sciences and Humanities Research Council of Canada. The study was made possible by this grant, which enabled me to engage in the research pursuit for a year, devoting my full-time with no other commitment.

I began this study through my own interest in exploring and pursuing the field work with the possibility of making it a major research project. Ellen Baar, a sociologist at York University, showed her keen interest in the project and joined me as a co-investigator in the stage of preparing the major part of the research. We collaborated in research design and in compiling the questionnaire. Activities in data collection and analysis were also jointly done.

Unfortunately, because of unforeseen circumstances, Ellen was unable to complete writing the chapters for the manuscript. After a delay of almost two years, I had no choice but to write it up by myself. I deeply regret both the delay in publication and the fact that co-authorship, as we had planned earlier, could not be realized.

I am indebted to Heather Martin, whose valuable editorial comments and suggested rewritings significantly improved the final manuscript.

This book, of course, would not have been possible without the support and co-operation of those people who took time from their working day to participate in this study. To all of them, JME workers on the floor, as well as management, both at the Canadian company and at the head office in Tokyo and Kyoto, I extend my sincere appreciation. While I am grateful to the members who participated in the study, they are not responsible for my findings.

Lastly, my best wishes for the future of the company are with all the members involved in it. It has been almost a year since I left the research site completely. Yet from bits of information which I have gathered here and there, I have a sense that things are going well; the plant is moving toward the "right direction."

Tomoko Makabe
Toronto.
April, 1989.

Introduction

Japanese investment in Canada grew rapidly during the 1970s, culminating in major investment projects in manufacturing throughout the 1980s. Today, nearly three hundred Japanese companies are expected to participate in a variety of manufacturing, merchandising, trading, banking and resource-related activities in Canada. In terms of Japan's total investment abroad, direct investment in particular, the Canadian share has remained small – approximately $2.5 billion in 1986-87, or about one-sixth the amount of Japanese investment in the United States. This amount is also less than one per cent of all foreign investment in Canada. Canada has not been an attractive market for Japanese corporations, which have traditionally viewed it as a northern extension of the American market. The investment projects by Japanese manufacturers are nonetheless important to Canada: they have provided new jobs and will continue to do so in the 1990s. Canada has a stake in these subsidiaries of Japanese firms, in their viability and in their future.[1]

The experience of Japanese firms in Canada has been a short one; unlike their American counterparts, they are relatively foreign to Canadians. Little is known about their organization and management practices. In fact, there is no systematic information on Japanese firms, manufacturing or otherwise, operating in Canada. This study is the first to examine in detail the internal operations of a Japanese-owned and managed factory in Canada.[2]

The study analyzes the transition of an electronic component manufacturing plant in a small town in Ontario from an American branch plant to a Japanese one. It focuses on the transformations resulting from the change in ownership of this organization, and attempts to arrive at a comprehensive understanding of the organization and of its behaviour during the period of transition. The study examines various factors to account for the increased productivity achieved, together with the difficulty that has been encountered by the new owner-company in redesigning a complex organization. It will assess both the success which has been achieved and the obstacles which remain almost four years after the Japanese-owned and managed plant began production in Canada.

In the past decade a considerable amount of research has examined Japanese subsidiaries doing business both in the United States and in Europe. Two of the studies, one done in Great Britain and the other in the United States, focussed specifically on Japanese manufacturing firms and Japanese production management. They have special relevance to the present study, which explores many of the same themes and issues and brings them up to date.

White and Trevor's study (1983) in Great Britain is the first attempt to examine comprehensively Japanese companies operating outside Japan. It endeavored to expand and elaborate the line of inquiry first undertaken by Takayamiya (1981) whose researches were conducted in Britain and elsewhere in Europe. These European studies indicated that Japanese firms operating in Europe tend not to introduce many of the features of so-called Japanese-style management, or if they do, to introduce them, only in a very watered-down form. Thus, for example, these studies found in Japanese subsidiaries no explicit system of lifetime employment, no company unions, no seniority-based payments system, no elaborate provisions for welfare or fringe benefits, no schemes for lifelong training, and no group decision-making process involving local employees. These findings, the researchers reported, applied equally to the manufacturing plants and to the financial firms. While Japanese firms were concerned about employment policy and personnel management in their foreign operations, the keynote has been a piecemeal pragmatism rather than attempting to introduce comprehensive Japanese systems of employment. These findings are, on the whole, consistent with those obtained by the present author's survey on Japanese-owned and managed sales firms doing business in Canada (Makabe, 1986).

The British studies also indicated that workers under Japanese management were not more satisfied with their employment than those in comparable British or American-owned companies. These studies have done little to support the notion advanced in the field for some time to explain the effectiveness of Japanese management: that Japanese practice depends on creating particularly "happy" or "contented" workers, or in generating particularly strong feelings among workers that human relations in the company are being given higher priority.

Yet the researchers emphasized that the Japanese-owned manufacturing firms were achieving very high levels of labour productivity and product quality in Europe. The point of the argument here is that the Japanese advantage lies in their organization of production work itself. Their method of production, located in the work place, and often consisting of relatively fine details, would be much less conspicuous than many features of Japanese employment systems which are popularly known. Examples of the type of work practices to which White and Trevor referred were an organized or orderly approach, an emphasis on details, an overriding priority attached to quality, and a punctilious sense of discipline. British workers saw these practices, the authors argued, as highly unusual and as giving their firms a great advantage.

Shimada and MacDuffies' (1987) recent review of the experience of Japanese automobile companies operating in the United States has shed further light on Japanese production management as well as on human resource management. This American study, based on field work at the production sites of all Japanese car manufacturers throughout the United States, documented that these Japanese companies have in general replicated almost exactly the hardware technology and production systems of their home country. Plant layout and design have closely followed the Japanese model. Most major production equipment and machines employed in Japan have been installed in American plants, according to Shimada and MacDuffie, and adjusted under the careful guidance and supervision of Japanese engineers.

The researchers identify "conspicuous technological features" of Japanese-owned and managed auto plants in the United States which are distinctively Japanese: they include quick feedback for quality assurance, a minimum inventory, the "pull" system of information flow and a just-in-time system, and reliance on human control as reflected in short set-up time for machines.[3]   The point of argument and of emphasis that Shimada and MacDuffie developed in their study is, however, that the Japanese uniqueness lies not in hardware technology alone, but in the interplay between technology and human resources that Japanese companies are attempting to introduce in their American plants.   The Japanese model of human resource management and industrical relations, the researchers maintain, characteristically features clearly structured jobs, a reward system and promotion ladder, joint decision-making, and training; and success or failure of the operation depends on how effectively these features are implemented.

The present Canadian study, which empirically examines the actual changes in organizational design which have occurred in the plant as a result of the transition from American to Japanese management, addresses four major questions. The first is, simply stated, how does Japanese production management differ in practice from American management? If two systems of management at the same plant using similar production processes, and producing the same products are significantly different from one another, then how exactly are they different and why? Secondly, how does the structure that the Japanese management introduced differ from the American structure? How are the division of work and the coordinating mechanisms different? What are the consequences of the changes for the number and kinds of managers and workers required?

The existing literature has not dealt systematically with the process of redesign or its consequences. Instead, it has suggested that Japanese plants operating overseas, as in the case of auto manufacturers in the United States, have attempted to replicate almost exactly the hardware technology and production systems of their home country, with some structural accommodations in response to cultural and environmental differences between North America and Japan. Despite these assumed differences, nonetheless, the general notion accepted in the field is that Japanese companies, i.e., Japanese-managed plants, operate like other functionally organized business firms. Very little reference has been made to the organizational design of Japanese firms operating outside Japan.

All of the questions elaborated by Mintzberg (1979) on the structuring of organizations are relevant to the present study: Did the American company have a taller structure while the Japanese have a flatter structure? Did the former company employ different control and coordination devices than its successor has?[4] Does the new management depend more extensively than did the former management on mutual adjustment, defining premises through training and indoctrination and standardizing the quality of outputs? Did the American structure depend more extensively on direct supervision and standardization of rules than the one designed by the Japanese? Is there more consultation within the Japanese-managed plant? And were communication flows within the American firm more regulated?

The electronics industry under investigation is characterized by rapid technological change, frequent product modification, and innovation. The dominant survival issue confronting the component manufacturing plant is the development of new and improved products and processes in a rapidly changing environment. Products often have to be changed as the needs of clients change. As a result, according to the theories fairly well established and empirically supported in the field, organizations can be expected to be more effective if they adopt organic, less formalized internal structures rather than structured, programmed and regulated structures and processes (Burns and Stalker, 1961).[5] Organizations must be flexible and adaptable. If, on the other hand, the manufacturing organization is to operate in a stable environment with little change and uncertainty, it would have a structure characterized by a set of what Burns and Stalker termed mechanistic design features. The organization would be formalized; it would extensively employ rules, procedures, and a clear hierarchy of authority. It would also be centralized, with most of the decisions made at the top. If the two organizations under comparison differ substantially in terms of their major design parameters, are design parameters within one organization more consistent with the technology and with market conditions than the other?

The critical contextual factors influencing the shape of the organizational structure, such as technology, environment, and economies of scale faced by the American-owned plant, are largely similar to the ones the Japanese are facing. The nature of the task in the component production system, including the actions, knowledge, and techniques used to change inputs into outputs, is the same everywhere, as there is only "one basic technology" to build components. Likewise, the elements outside the boundary of the organization are almost identical. Industry, government, suppliers, customers, and the financial community surrounding the plant are not dissimilar to any marked degree between the two operations. The fact that the owner of the plant is foreign, coming from outside, and the plant is formerly an American-multinational corporation and now a Japanese counterpart, also provides a common ground for comparison. As 'foreigners' they both have to relate to the Canadian environment.

Thus, this study addresses an important theoretical question: does productivity increase when manufacturing industries change the modes of achieving standardization, unit size, administrative size, methods of supervision and coordination? Until now no one in the field has systematically and empirically gathered evidence to prove or disprove this question.

If overseas Japanese management does not produce greater worker satisfaction or rely on distinctive employment-personnel policies and provisions, and if working conditions in Japanese firms are not better than in non-Japanese firms, as the previous studies indicate, then something else must contribute to productivity. Shimada and MacDuffie have created the term "humanware" – the technological linkage between the production system and human resources – as a contributing factor in explaining the Japanese performance in the auto industry in the United States. The present study may be able to assess the design factors which affect some aspects of a branch plant operating in this country, including the differential productivity (if this exists in the plant under investigation).

The second area of inquiry concerns itself with the process of transition of the organization. This process happens to be a somewhat rocky one for the period of our investigation, and thus this study is not the one to present as a case of a 'success story'. What obstacles did the newly arrived company experience in effecting a transition from American to Japanese management and what difficulties do workers experience making the transition?

Typically, the introduction of Japanese management in manufacturing enterprises everywhere outside Japan to this point has occurred by replicating Japanese design of production processes and employing individuals with little previous employment experience, that is to say, unconstrained introduction of Japanese management. These conditions are regarded as 'prerequisites' of running Japanese plants outside Japan. Studies of the success of Japanese plants have asked whether an integrated package of Japanese practices can be transported effectively across cultures. The success of these companies has suggested that cultural differences are not a major impediment to the acceptance of packages of Japanese production practices by non-Japanese. Yet, very little has been learned about the actual process through which increased productivity is achieved. The current study looks at the nature of constraints accepted by the company and consequences of the acceptance – obstacles and difficulties faced by both the company and worker – when an American-owned plant declared redundant by its head office during a recession is reopened under Japanese management.

Through the process of probing the constrained introduction of Japanese management at the Canadian plant, it can be discerned exactly how American and Japanese management differ. The differences in assumptions in production work will be articulated in an attempt to lead to some insight into the nature of the discordance between Japanese and American management. Although the transition to Japanese management within the plant remains unfinished, this study has afforded the researcher an opportunity to study the consequences of decoupling the technical and human components which are, as argued by Shimada and MacDuffie, usually tightly integrated in Japanese management systems. This will enable us to better discern the contribution made by each to productivity improvements.

The third question of this study deals with the worker reaction to organizational and managerial change. It will examine empirically workers' perceptions of Japanese management as they experience it. The roles of worker, supervisor, and manager change as a result of the transition from one to another and of the process through which quality and productivity are aimed to affect an increase in the production system. How do Canadian workers accept roles defined by new management? How do Canadian workers perceive techniques and work practices introduced by Japanese management and evaluate the effectiveness of such techniques and practices? Are the changes introduced in the production processes, coordination and supervision sensible in the eyes of Canadian workers? Do their perceptions differ from British workers (as examined by White and Trevor) in any significant way? Under Japanese management, supervisors have a very different role. How are they adjusting to increased responsibilities imposed upon them by the new management and coping with the role conflict and ambiguity which they normally experience? Is the increased discretion perceived as desirable by the Canadian supervisors?

We are going to measure worker satisfaction, and the priority assigned to employment security by Canadian workers. The worker's views and attitudes on employment security is especially significant and meaningful in light of the new management's commitment to the unofficially stated policy of no lay-off. How significant to the workers is this management commitment? Are they more concerned with employment security or with potential mobility outside the organization? What is the role of employment security in promoting acceptance of Japanese management?

Fourthly and lastly, the study assesses the constrained introduction of Japanese management. The constraints that the case company has had to accommodate in undertaking the business enterprise are essential in shaping the structure of the organization: the company purchased a factory and machinery designed by the former owner rather than by itself. It accepted a Canadian government loan and grant and, in return, agreed to keep the regular work force intact and to recognize the existing union and the overall institutional framework of labour-managment relations which had been previously established. The company further agreed to recall workers on the basis of seniority, and started the operation with a work force largely consisting of those recalled workers. What do these constraints mean to the organization in redesigning its structure? If increased productivity at the Canadian plant is less than expected, or workers do not evaluate the Japanese approach positively, or conflict between employer and employees increases rather than decreases, then it may be that redesign in response to constraints results in transforming the innovation, with a smaller increase in productivity than otherwise. The problems encountered by the company in taking over an existing North American plant may have useful implications not only for other Japanese firms thinking of establishing branch plants in North America, but for their potential partners, including employees, trade unions, various levels of government and suppliers. What do all the concerned parties learn from the experience of the company, the first manufacturer involved in production activity in a substantial way in this country?

The following pseudonyms will be used for the rest of the manuscript: 'Simcoe Bay' is used for the town where the plant is located; 'Japanese Manufacturing Enterprise,' or 'JME' for short, is referred to for the new company, a Japanese manufacturing firm from Tokyo, while the former owner of the plant, a New York-based multinational corporation, is referred to as 'Arcan'; the products manufactured by this plant are identified merely as 'electronic components' instead of using the commonly used product name.

This manuscript comprises an introduction and nine chapters. In the first two chapters we provide background information on the study; how the information for the study was obtained and how the takeover of the business enterprise took place. All the methods used in data collection and in data analysis for the present study are outlined in the following chapter after this introduction.

A few words in justifying and defending the methodology of case study (Becker, 1971) are in order here. This is a case study of an organization. It attempts, first and foremost, to grasp the overall picture of the organization under two different managements. It also deals with a variety of descriptive and theoretical issues. Some of the issues presented in the course of analysis and discussion are, the author believes, of major importance, touching on crucial aspects of the structure and processes of organization in general, however limited the applicability of the findings may be. Empirical data obtained from this study is also important in filling the vacancy in the existing body of research in the country where no systematic information exists on Japanese organizations at all. Thus, the reasons for undertaking this study are almost exclusively empirical. No attempts are made to wrestle with theoretical issues in any systematic way or even to generate hythpotheses which could be tested in another study. Like many other well-done case studies in the field, therefore, there are weaknesses in the way this study is conducted. It makes it difficult to generalize the findings. The difficulty of replication is problematical in terms of the validity of conclusions.

In Chapter Two, a brief profile of the community where the enterprise is situated, and of the workers who are the residents of the community and members of the enterprise, is presented. Also, we introduce here the focal organization by way of providing information on the parent companies, that is, the owners of the Canadian subsidiary: when and why the former owner-company came to the area of the province to build a branch plant and how it quit the operation some twenty years later; and the successor's reasoning behind taking over the business once considered redundant.

Chapter Three is the first presentation and analysis of our empirical data. It looks at the physical framework of the organization by comparing organizational charts of the respective companies and outlines the changes in organizational design which have occurred as a result of the transition from American to Japanese ownership. Substantial differences in terms of the major design parameters and consequent staffing and manpower policies are noted. Differences between the two organizations in terms of the priority attached to functional activities are also empirically assessed.

In Chapter Four, changes in the job structure focussing on classification, rotation and seniority are discussed. In an attempt to restructure the job-related system within the plant, there are three crucial issues that the new management tackled: 1) gaining acceptance of a single job classification within operators' ranks in replacing the existing multi-leveled classification system; 2) rotating jobs among operators as well as among skilled workers and technicians; and 3) getting rid of rules of seniority as a primary determinant in layoffs, job assignments and promotion. While management attempts to introduce and implement the Japanese model, the North American perspectives on job classifications, rotation and seniority prevail persistently among employees. Other problems related to work customs and practices will also be touched upon in this section of the report.

The topic of Chapter Five is supervision in production. The discussion focusses on the impact of technology on roles and duties performed by the supervisor, the critical figure in supervision. The notion to be developed in the course of the discussion is that technology changes the role of the supervisor, and that as technology changes, the role must change too. The problem to be assessed here is whether or not Canadian supervisors adequately understand the consequences of technological change on their roles, and are aware of differences in assumptions between American and Japanese management and supervision. The orientation and skills required to perform the supervisory function in accordance to the assumptions of Japanese management are quite differenct from those required under the assumptions of American management.

Chapter Six examines differences in interpretation and assumptions between the two very different methods of quality control used at the plant. Failure to understand the differences can result in strain on the people involved in the operation. The differences between the two is demonstrated by comparing the respective approaches to ensuring the quality of the product, and by analyzing worker reaction to the transition from North American quality control to Japanese-style quality assurance. Since the new Japanese management introduced some but not all elements of the approach to achieving quality used in their Canadian plant, this chapter also assesses the consequences of partial implementation. Our analysis will emphasize the importance to the Japanese approach of the fit between automated technology and the design of the management system.

Chapter Seven deals with worker satisfaction (or dissatisfaction) with employment. Canadian workers' ratings of their own satisfaction or dissatisfaction with various aspects of their employment are compared with those of British counterparts. Job security, pay and working conditions are the areas of greatest contrast and are analyzed in detail. The problem of motivation of employees is tied in with such aspects of jobs as training and promotion, which are said to be the "survival matter" for Japanese manufacturing firms operating outside Japan. The Canadian plant cannot be an exception. We argue that creating a reasonable structure with new promotional opportunities tied to retraining are the most urgent matters for both management and labour involved in the plant operation.

In the final chapter of analysis we examine some of the issues in foreign-ownership using the present case plant as a focal point. In Canada the consequences of foreign ownership have been debated for some time. In this chapter the specific issues analyzed are the degree of "truncation" in the branch plant under the two managements and the degree of autonomy the plant was exercising under American ownership and management. These topics reflect on the legacy of American investment in this country and we question whether American-owned management, the management structure and style it created, was sensitive enough or not to the need for change and advancing the skills and experience required to redesign the product and marketing.

The report concludes with a summary of findings and implications of the study.

Notes

1. In the past few years Japanese investment in Canada has undergone considerable transformation, moving to financial investment in a form of loans and securities, as the strong yen began to drive an enormous transfer of wealth from North America to Asia. In just three years Japan has become almost as large a lender to Canada as the United States, with $42.1 billion in bonds and loans to Canadian federal and provincial governments, compared with $45 billion from the United States, through the end of 1987.

2. Two surveys on Japanese business in Canada were conducted in the past: 1) Richard Wright, *The Elusive Alliance - Japanese Business in Canada.* (Montreal: The Institute of Research and Public Policy, 1984); 2) Tomoko Makabe, *Japanese-Owned and Managed Businesses in Canada,* working paper #28 (Toronto: Toronto-York Joint Centre on Modern East Asia, York University, 1984).

3. The most systematic and detailed explanation of the leading model of Japanese production system, namely the Toyota production system, can be obtained from Monden (1983), *Toyota Production System: Practical Approach to Production Management.* See the reference for the source.

4. Mintzberg notes five coordinating mechanisms in explaining the ways in which organizations coordinate work processes: mutual adjustment, direct supervision, and standardization of work processes: work outputs, and worker skills. As organizational work becomes more complicated, the favoured means of coordination generally shifts from mutual adjustment to direct supervision to standardization.

5. Throughout the manuscript such terms as *bureaucratic, mechanistic, closed, formalized,* and *structured* are interchangeably used in describing the structure of an organization at one end, in contrast to the *organic, open, flexible, less formalized,* and *adaptable* structure at the other end. The original term of organic versus mechanistic structure was elaborated on in their study on industrial firms by Burns and Stalker (1961).

Chapter One
Methodology of the Study

The present study is a case study of an industrial organization. It focusses on the transformations resulting from the change in ownership of this organization, and attempts to arrive at a comprehensive understanding of the organization and of its behaviour during the period of transition.

The organization on which the present analysis is based was largely in the developmental stage at the time when the major part of the research was conducted, and continues to be. The new management of the Simcoe Bay plant has been in the process of importing and introducing JME's Japanese style and method of production management to its Canadian plant. Over the period of almost four years since the company took over the plant, it has been changing the organizational structure and existing policies incrementally and has been developing new ones. These changes will continue for some years to come.

The initial task in this study was to determine whether the plant under Japanese management is really applying distinctive policies and practices. If this was established empirically, it would then be possible to pose questions about how this process takes place, and about the legitimization of Japanese-style management in the eyes of Canadian workers.

To demonstrate the distinctiveness of a Japanese employment-management system, some method of comparison with policies and practices in other companies was needed. The most common method would have been to match and compare at least two organizations, one under Japanese management and the other under North American management. In reality, however, not a single Canadian- or American-owned manufacturing firm in the area concerned is sufficiently similar to the present case to permit useful comparison. (As a matter of fact, there is no other manufacturing plant operating in Canada producing this form of electronic component.) Thus, it was technically impossible to assess the differences in Japanese and Canadian production management between two similar firms, and equally impossible to have an internal comparison, that is, to use another Japanese - owned and managed manufacturing firm, which was similar enough in terms of production process and the size of factory as a control group.

Instead, the present study compares the Canadian experience to the British findings of White and Trevor (1984). To facilitate the comparison, a set of key questions used in the British study dealing with working practices, employee satisfaction, human relations management indicators, and worker reactions to management, was employed.

In addition, since most of the plant workers (eighty-five per cent of the operators at the time when data were collected) have experienced both the Arcan and the JME systems of management at the same plant in the same production process, a comparison could be made of workers' perceptions of the differences. A major source of data for this study[1] has thus been a questionnaire completed by the workers themselves and supplemented by in-depth interviews with representative groups of workers at the plant. These personal interviews have provided details of the differences between Arcan and JME. They cover the following areas: definitions of work processes; evaluations of management methods at Arcan and JME and some consequences of these methods; evaluations of the incentive system, of training and opportunities for mobility, and of the approach to supervision and human relations at Arcan and JME; the degree of planning and coordination of work processes at Arcan and JME; opportunities to affect decisions at Arcan and JME; worker proposals for changing JME; and an evaluation of distinctive JME practices including job rotation, individual responsibility to quality control, shift meetings and shift overlapping. As a result of these interviews it became possible to make a very full comparison between workers' experiences of and reaction to the Japanese organization and style of management and their reassessment of the American type of management used by their former employer.

The topics covered in the questionnaire were the mobility workers experienced within Arcan and their evaluation of opportunities for mobility within JME, individuals' occupational histories and definitions of a good job to measure inter-firm mobility experiences, their preferences for staying with one employer or moving among employers, and the weight assigned by them to different components of a good job. The questionnaires also provided information on the social background of employees. Since the questions on supervisors and organizational assessment were taken from a Canadian study on workplace democracy by Nightingale (1982), the responses obtained from this study thus can be compared with those from the Canadian study.

The senior management of JME promised active support to the researcher involved in the present study, who approached the company soon after its production activities became substantial. The management indicated its interest in knowing both the workers' reactions to the Japanese company and their receptiveness to the changes that the company wanted to implement in the plant. At about the same time the researcher approached the local union and got a fairly positive response to the proposed study, union executives showed an interest in the study and agreed to encourage their members to participate in it.

The Questionnaires (Worker)

A questionnaire was distributed to every hourly-rated, permanently employed worker on the shop floor as of the second week of May, 1986. At that time JME had in its employ a total of four hundred twenty-one production workers, including both permanent and casual employees, those in the plant and those on leave of absence; of these, two hundred forty-four (fifty-eight per cent) were men and one hundred seventy-seven (forty-two per cent) were women. A total of three hundred ninety-eight permanent workers were asked to take part in the study and to fill in the questionnaire. On May 16, 1986 each worker received the questionnaire together with his/her paycheque. Attached were a letter from the researchers requesting the members' cooperation and assistance, and a supporting letter written by the president of the local union.[2] The researchers' letter explained the general nature of the study, that participation in the study was voluntary, that individual responses would be anonymous, and that a summary report of the study would be given to the union for all the members to see. Workers were asked to complete the questionnaire and return it by dropping it in a box placed in the cafeteria. The questionnaire typically required thirty to forty-five minutes to complete. (Both the questionnaire and the letters attached are included in the Appendix.)

One reminder notice was passed on through the supervisors to those who had not returned the questionnaire by the end of the third week. By July 1, the last day of the collection, two hundred forty-eight questionnaires had been returned, of which seven were either completely blank or largely spoiled. The response ratio was 62.3 per cent.

The two hundred forty-one respondents used in the analysis of this study consist of almost equal numbers of men (121) and women (120). Thus, the group contains more women proportionately than does the actual population of the work force. The bias caused by this over representation by women in the sample has resulted in a higher proportion of respondents in certain work areas within the plant, notably in the front sections where jobs are in large part physically light ones and tend to be performed by women. In the back end of the plant, on the other hand, the jobs generally require more physical strength, including some heavy lifting, and tend to be occupied by men. The difference in gender-based job experiences on the shop floor may have had some impact on the response to certain questions raised in the questionnaire.

There are several possible reasons why some workers decided not to participate in the survey. The first might possibly be that the questions, open-ended ones in particular, placed a burden on respondents whose mother tongue was not English. The work force at the JME plant, judging from their surnames, contains a fair proportion (approximately one-third of the total) of people of French origin. No question was provided that would give information about the native language of the employees, and thus there is no way of assessing fairly the level of literacy (writing skills) which may well have produced the negative or passive attitudes toward the study shown by some employees. Equally, negative attitudes may have arisen from a fear, at least among some workers, of job loss as a result of participation in the study. That such fears were prevalent among some workers was reported to the researchers by supervisors and respondents during the course of the interviews.

The Interviews (Worker)

Upon completion of the questionnaire a total of one hundred twenty-six workers, about a third of the work force, were contacted for an interview. These people were randomly selected from the employee list-of-the-week compiled by the company, in order to have a cross-section of respondents representative of fourteen work departments. Thus, a variety of job experience could be considered. Twenty people refused to be interviewed, and sixteen were not available for various reasons. Thus, altogether, ninety hourly-rated workers became interviewee-respondents to whom a $5 honorarium was paid. The management was very cooperative in organizing these interviews. Most of the interviews were conducted by the researchers in offices within the plant before and after the workers' shifts, while a few workers, most of whom were on leave of absence, were interviewed in their homes. The interview usually took about half an hour.

In the interview, respondents were asked to describe in their own words the main features of their employment. The open-ended questions given in the questionnaire were clarified and elaborated on by the respondents, some in a fair amount of detail. The discussions lent themselves to a more qualitative and richer type of interpretation of key questions of the study. Thus, direct quotations either from the interviews or the comments given on the open-ended questions are used as widely as possible in the process of data analysis. The qualitative statements are, nonetheless, used to back up the salient line of the findings established by the statistical evidence. In that sense the qualitative data are supplementary and contributory.

The Interviews and Questionnaires (Manager and Supervisor)

A structured questionnaire similar to the one used for workers was also distributed to supervisors and to some salaried staff members, technicians and engineers. All of the supervisors in production, sixteen in number at the time the research was conducted, and all ex-Arcan employees were interviewed in the same manner as the workers.

The main providers of information on the JME operation of the plant included such senior management as the president, the plant manager, the production manager, and the manager of industrial relations. A few Japanese expatriates, mainly engineering staff, were also rather informally interviewed in Japanese (all the quotations used in this report from the interviews conducted in Japanese were translated into English by the researcher, the author of this manuscript). In conversations with the researcher they gave their views on various aspects of the plant operation. Discussions with JME personnel were semi-structured in the sense that, while questions were provided prior to the interview on some occasions, they were largely informal and wide-ranging. The informants revealed much useful information about such topics as the day-to-day operation of the factory, the differences between Arcan and JME work processes, the relationships between the parent company and the subsidiary, and, finally, their perceptions of the company's overall performance.

The Canadian plant reports to the head office of JME in Tokyo. All the business reports are addressed to the Director of International Operations. The plant has close links to the Kyoto Works, one of JME's many production facilities, which provides all the designs and development of the product to the Canadian plant, except for the application designs which the Canadian plant itself does. The division of component products within the Kyoto Works in JME's organization chart belongs to the Consumer Products Group of the corporation. This division provides all the necessary information about marketing and managerial-administrative assistance to the Canadian plant. The researcher had an opportunity to visit both the Kyoto plant and the corporate head office in Tokyo in the summer of 1986. The discussions with the Japan-based personnel involved in the Canadian operation became another source of information for this study. They provided interpretations of data obtained from the Canadian personnel, an evaluation of the success already achieved by JME, and an assessment of the obstacles still to be overcome.

Lastly, the information on Arcan's operation of the plant, its organizational structure as well as its management methods, was obtained mostly from ex-managers of Arcan and from union executives. The five ex-managers available for interviews in the early stages of the study discussed with the researcher various aspects of the plant operation and became very useful informants. The topics covered in these discussions included the background on the plant closure, Arcan business policy, relations between the plant and the head office, the organizational-structural measures used, manpower-staffing policies, personnel provisions, job tenure and labour turnover, work practices on the shop floor, and "problems" in quality, management and productivity. The office of public relations of the Canadian head office also provided such factual information as the organization chart of the plant and other company documents.

8

Notes

1. The data base for this study is workers, supervisors, and technical-managerial staff on the floor, and employees of JME who are actively involved in the work of production. The salaried employees, those who are outside of the "operating core," namely, the support staff in the office, are not included in the study, as the central theme of the study concerns itself with production management.

2. This study was initiated by Tomoko Makabe, the author of this manuscript, as a continuation of her previous study on Japanese businesses in Canada, and received funding from the Social Sciences and Humanities Research Council of Canada. Ellen Baar, a sociologist at York University, joined the project at this stage and collaborated with Makabe in finalizing the research design and compiling the questionnaire. The field work in the early stage was pursued by Makabe alone, while later data collection activities were jointly done, dividing the tasks between the two. Because Baar failed to complete writing of the chapters for the manuscript, for various reasons, Makabe has undertaken to write it up. Thus, in the following chapters, the identification of researcher is either as singular or a pair, depending on the specific activity concerned.

Chapter Two
Background of the Study

Background to the JME Takeover of Arcan

The Simcoe Bay area, including the surrounding small communities, has a resident year-round population of 35,000 composed of 11,500 households. This population results in a total work force of approximately 16,000, which is heavily dependent on manufacturing (40 per cent of the total labour force, as compared to 24 per cent of Ontario as a whole).[1]

The town has a varied light industrial base. There are about sixty firms, most of which are small establishments. They are widely diverse in their manufactured products, producing, among other items, parts for automobiles, industrial fabrics, cameras and sailboats. The two largest employers in the area, however, consist of a manufacturer of electronic components and an auto-parts plant, both of which are foreign-owned companies. Many of the town's workers have had some contact with one or the other, or even with both of them at one time or other, and thus have "gotten used to working with outsiders."

Historically the area has experienced considerable fluctuation in its economic fortunes due to the difficulties in attracting and maintaining a stable industrial base and to the seasonal nature of its tourist-based employment. The problems associated with an unstable and weak economic base were underlined in 1982 when Arcan, the area's second largest employer with approximately nine hundred employees, closed its electronic-component manufacturing plant.

Arcan had come to Simcoe Bay in 1966, when the Canadian government actively encouraged the company to open an electronic-component manufacturing plant. The federal government's policy was to provide loans to companies who would invest in economically stagnant areas. Arcan's investment in the Simcoe Bay plant represented the largest ever made in the Canadian electronics industry. The plant was designed to serve the Canadian market and, when it made economic sense to do so, the European market. In its earlier years, when the plant was getting off the ground, it was not always profit-making due to "some quality problems." Nonetheless, the company became increasingly successful throughout its years of operation. One of the ex-managers of Arcan interviewed for this study said that there is no way Arcan could have failed had it wanted to continue to be a presence in Canada. This view was shared by practically everybody in the town of Simcoe Bay.

When the plant was first established, Arcan was the world leader in the manufacture of electronic components, and it continued to have a stranglehold on the industry until the late 1970s. Then the technological advances from the Far East, particularly from Japan, threatened Arcan's market. In response to the threat, Arcan made significant investments in its Canadian plant. Not too long before the announcement of the closure, it invested $5 million in order to achieve the economies of scale that were necessary in order to meet the price demands of the marketplace, both Canadian and foreign. These investments brought the capacity of the plant, operating on a three-shift base, to nearly one million components a year (at an average pace of 4,000 units a day). After the technical capacity was attained, however, this level of production was never realized due to the softening of market conditions.[2] When the market went soft the "peaking plant"[3] was closed so that funds could be diverted to modernization of the company's U.S. plants.

Just before the closure, the company was struggling to adapt to its lessening share of the world market in the midst of the 1981-82 recession. Even if its markets had been sustained during the recession, however, the plant would have required additional capital investment to remain competitive. Those responsible for the management of the plant went to Ottawa for federal help, asking $9 million to re-tool the equipment.[4] This was an attempt to salvage the plant and save at least six hundred jobs. The application for the grant was refused by the federal government and, because of this, the company decided not to spend any more money for further reorganization. In the view of the head office, the long-term prospects were not good enough to keep the Canadian plant in operation. "The loss of the company's European market, which had accounted for more than forty per cent of the plant's products, a general softening of demand in Canada and the rest of North America, and a severe foreign price competition"[5] encouraged the company to close the plant. The export-based activity depended on currency fluctuations and the volume of business was inadequate to stimulate backward linkages. The decision to close was made at head office in July, 1982, and the actual closing took place in December of that year. According to local observers it was a "wrong," "careless," and "short-sighted" decision; not very long after the closure of the plant the market began to turn around.

The town was shaken when it found out that $27 million in payroll would be lost as a result of the plant closing. This, together with the shutdown of several other smaller firms, resulted in an unemployment rate in excess of thirty per cent during the 1981-1982 recession period.[6] The town decided to work actively to find a new owner somewhere in the world who would acquire the component-manufacturing plant. The local union took the initiative and provided $5,000 for a study to assess the feasibility of reopening the plant.[7] The town spent six months actively searching for a new owner for the plant before it found what seemed to be an ideal candidate in JME, a Japanese firm seeking to broaden its base in North America.[8]

JME has been one of Japan's leading manufacturers of electrical equipment since its founding in 1921. A well-established company, today it is a full-range manufacturer of electrical and electronic products, from giant power generators to semiconductors, with annual sales of $8.1 billion (U.S.), involving some seventy thousand employees in Japan and overseas.[9] The company established itself as a multinational company during the 1970s, and now boasts subsidiaries and joint ventures operating in thirty-three countries, with thirty-four factories in Japan as well.

Both the Japanese and Canadian governments encouraged JME to establish a plant in Canada. For some time the Japanese government had been urging major industries to establish plants in the markets they served. Production operations in Canada were expected to soothe Canadian hostility towards products imported from Japan. The argument was that production plants within Canada would not only provide visible job opportunities for Canadians, but would also permit the importation from Japan to Canada of semi-finished parts and components rather than finished products, making Japan far less vulnerable to dumping charges.

In order to keep up with the growing world market, furthermore, the company needed to expand its total production capabilities. An additional production site in North America had become increasingly attractive economically due to the gradual appreciation of the yen since 1983. This has become even more of an incentive since then. The value of the Japanese currency appreciated forty per cent against the U.S. dollar during the first six months of 1986 and a further fifty per cent toward the end of 1987. As a result, products manufactured in Japan are losing their degree of cost competitiveness.

The problems of trade imbalance accumulated over the years between the United States and Japan (and to a lesser extent Canada) have also become more acute in recent years. Investment in North America helps to solve this problem by providing a potential escape from existing exportation constraints for highly export-oriented Japanese companies, including JME. JME had already established a small share in the Canadian market by exporting its Japan-made products. It had also established a manufacturing plant in California, and has been operating a semiconductor plant in South Carolina for some years. It, therefore, felt confident that a production base in Canada could be immediately utilized to further penetrate the North American market by placing familiar products in established distribution channels.

The decision to purchase the Simcoe Bay plant made by the parent company of JME was based on the belief that it could compete in world markets serviced by the Canadian plant. JME selected the Simcoe Bay plant because it would enable the company to begin production immediately rather than spending a year and a half designing and establishing a new facility. The firm expected as well to benefit from an experienced work force and to increase its expertise by taking over a plant which had been operated by a company with the greatest share of the North American market. Arcan was viewed by the Japanese as "an excellent company in certain areas such as the development of new technology – the invention of something completely new; their competitive strength is in originating and creating something new." As a result, taking over their plant and their employees, together with loans that the provincial and federal governments were prepared to provide, was an attractive prospect.

The workers who were laid off when the Arcan plant closed in December, 1982, were rehired when JME purchased the plant. JME preferred, initially at least, to keep as many Arcan managers and workers as needed. This was, of course, favourably received by every party involved in the transfer transactions. The initial contract signed between JME and the Communications, Electronic, Electrical, Technical and Salaried Workers of Canada provided that JME would use Arcan's seniority list for recall purposes. For every ten Arcan employees rehired, JME could hire one new employee. For the first two years of the operation, however, the company recruited not a single new hourly worker. By the end of the third year, slightly less than fifteen per cent of the work force were newly hired members of JME; the rest were former Arcan operators.

JME's first Simcoe Bay contract with the union was signed in July, 1985. In this labour contract, the company confirmed its commitment to the work force it had hired by stating that it would "make every effort to avoid layoffs" and would "maintain regular crews." To attain these ends, however, it requested that a new category of employees, "casual employees," be created to fill temporary positions, such as temporary peak load employees and replacements for people on leave of absence.[10] In return for job security endorsed by the management, the union agreed to this new category of workers.

Thus, it may be argued that JME chose a constrained approach to the introduction of Japanese management to its Canadian plant. Specifically, the company accepted government loans, agreed to employ Arcan workers and to work with the existing union, recalled workers on the basis of seniority, and purchased a factory and machinery designed by Arcan rather than JME.

A few months after the new owner took over the operation, the world market for electronic components turned around and has been growing steadily ever since (with the exception of the seasonal downturn each year). This has been a great advantage to the company. The plant started working a single shift in April, 1984, moved to two in June, and to three shifts by October. Less than a year later four hundred seventy employees were producing thirty to thirty-five hundred components a day, a level of productivity equal to that of the former owner. In the summer of 1986, when data were collected for the present study, the plant was producing forty-one hundred units a day, the highest level ever achieved, and was exporting sixty-five to seventy per cent of its products.

At the corporate level, JME's world market share is currently about seven per cent.[11] The corporation aims to expand its share up to ten per cent by 1990. In order to achieve this goal, the Simcoe Bay plant is expected to double its present level of production.

The Workers at the Simcoe Bay Plant: Profile

Hourly-rated workers at the Simcoe Bay plant can be classified into three main skill levels. The most highly skilled and thus the highest-paid are the tradesmen or maintenance men, fourteen of them altogether, who are all workers with apprenticeships or comparable training. These men are machine setters and repairmen who are concerned with servicing machines and equipment. They work independently throughout the plant.

The machine attendants, called utility workers, constitute another group of workers who are relatively highly skilled. The thirty-one utility men are all ex-Arcan employees with long years of service. In general, they have not had any lengthy training but have picked up over the years the particular skill which their present jobs require. These men work as machine attendants in any of the fourteen departments where, together with the operators (the lowest-skilled workers), they are engaged in the manufacture of components.

The rest of the workers are semi-skilled. They are production workers who perform jobs which usually call for only short training periods. Work tasks performed in the fourteen different production processes and departments range from the initial task of handling raw material to the packing and delivery of the finished products. There are slight differences in the skills and knowledge required to perform these tasks, and wages are to some extent differentiated accordingly. Currently, there are nineteen job categories differentiated by the wage received. These range from the poorest paid jobs in the front section of the plant, in general the least physically demanding and regarded as easiest to perform, to the highest paid jobs in the back section. It is generally accepted among workers from Arcan days that the more physically demanding the job is, the harder it is, and thus it should be rewarded accordingly.

The respondent group in these three categories, is aged from 22 to 64, the average being 38, or 38.4 to be precise. This figure is significantly higher than the average of 36 years for the national-industrial group, and for good reason.[12] JME's manning policy sought to make use of the existing expertise, and thus to hire as many ex-Arcan workers as needed. In accordance with the arrangement made with the union, recalling of hourly-rated workers was done on the basis of the seniority the workers had earned with Arcan. This practice resulted in the hiring of a relatively older group whose tenure with Arcan averaged ten years. This job tenure figure is also significantly higher than the national-industrial average group.[13] Thus, the average age of the group of ex-Arcan workers is 40, while that of the group of newly hired workers is 26. This contrast reflects management's preference for hiring younger workers in general and its effort to expand the proportion of young workers. Nevertheless, a large majority of the workers on the shop floor are middle-aged men and women, not much different in average age and length of service from their supervisors and managers.

Sixty-nine per cent of the workers at the Simcoe Bay plant are married and living with spouse and children. The majority (sixty-seven per cent) of those who are married, separated or divorced have two or more dependent children and are heavily burdened with financial demands and responsibilities.

An average plant worker earned a wage of $404.20 per week as of July, 1986. Hourly rates ranged from $8.19 an hour for semi-skilled workers to $12.00 for tradesmen. Annual earnings are estimated to be approximately $19,000 (with the extra income from overtime the amount would be $20,000-$23,000 in 1985-86). According to JME workers themselves and people outside the company, these wages are above-average in the community of Simcoe Bay.

Workers at the Simcoe Bay plant are very likely to be natives of the area and seem closely attached to their present employment as well as to their family and community. Nearly six out of ten respondents were born in the area; seven out of ten have grown up either in the town or its surrounding areas. The workers completed an average of 10.7 years of schooling or the equivalent of two-and-a-half years of high school; one out of five respondents completed less than nine years of schooling. Among the newly employed group with no experience of having the previous employer, the average number of years completed is twelve years, or the equivalent of a high school education, the standard level of education for that age group.

Prior to coming to work at the plant, the average number of previous jobs held by the respondent group was 1.6. Ex-Arcan employees were likely to have come to work at the plant in the early 1970s, after working at one or two jobs elsewhere. Most previous jobs were with firms not too far from the Bay area. Those who had some experience working outside the area usually returned to the Bay when they married or started a family. During their working lives workers have been confined to unskilled or semi-skilled jobs, largely in manual employment, in small-scale industry, in agriculture, and in distributive and other services. Looking at their 'career' history, the workers at the plant can be regarded as being less mobile, geographically as well as occupationally, than other workers employed in similar industries in other parts of the province. They are in tune with the firm: a large majority of them believe, as the evidence from the questionnaire in later chapters reveals, that it is better to stay with the same firm for a long time than to move around to get ahead, and thus they expect to be with the same firm in many years' time. Workers feel at the same time discouraged from leaving, because they have invested in the plant "for too long," and have consequently earned rights of seniority. They are unlikely to get a better job elsewhere under the prevailing labour market conditions, in the Bay area in particular, which may be another factor making them less mobile.

Recruitment at Arcan was dependent on the practice of hiring from a pool of applicants recommended by employees, typically their relatives and friends. Thus, for many of the workers, workmates at the plant are also fairly important 'significant others.' The recruitment method widely practised at Arcan, and the homogeneity of background characteristics described above, encourage workers to develop close relationships with fellow workers either within or outside the plant. In fact many get involved in tightly knit social networks based on kinship, and this personal association is cited as a major source of satisfaction in life.

Workers' strong commitment to family, workmates, friends, and the community parallels their close attachment to their present employment. A majority of respondents indicated that they were not thinking of changing jobs in the near future. The single most important factor in weighing job offers, when and if they come, is the security of the job, which is more important than all other factors including the pay. Details of the discussion on these issues will be presented in a later chapter.

Notes

1. Economic Development Committee, Town of Simcoe Bay, *An Economic Development Strategy for Simcoe Bay*, June 1984, p. 127.

2. Information provided by a former employee of Arcan during personal interview.

3. The term is used for a type of plant owned by a multinational. They are expected to serve domestic as well as overseas markets only when it is sensible to do so in accordance with the strategic marketing plans of the corporation.

4. Information provided by a former employee.

5. Local newspaper published in Simcoe Bay, July 16, 1982.

6. Report of Economic Development Committee, op. cit., p. 1.

7. The feasibility study was conducted by a firm in Toronto. It cost $40,000, the difference being chipped in by the federal and provincial governments.

8. Despite the reopening of the plant, the level of unemployment in the area has remained substantially higher than the provincial average.

9. The Company Business Report of JME, 1986.

10. The use of "casual" or "temporary" employees is one of the manpower practices unique to the Japanese employment system (Dore, 1973). The Japanese system, offering workers long-term career prospects, pensions, and welfare measures designed to provide long-term work incentives, has to have an element of flexibility to adjust to short-term business fluctuations. Temporary or part-time workers, who are not admitted to the enterprise family, are dismissible whenever times are bad, and thus they offer the necessary flexibility.

11. Information provided by JME management.

12. *Census of Canada 1981*, pp. 920-921, Table 4.

13. Statistics Canada, *The Labour Force Survey*, 1986.

Chapter Three

Changes in Organization and Structure

The component manufacturing plant under investigation is situated in the industrial section of the town of Simcoe Bay. The twenty-year-old building standing in the suburban open space looks solid and fine with the new company insignia emblazoned in red on it. The company insignia, although conspicuous enough, is the only evidence that indicates the new owner of the plant. JME has added few Japanese features to the appearance of the plant with the exception of the customary ornaments of Japanese arts and crafts displayed in the reception area inside the building.

On the shop floor as well, little change has been made to the physical design established by Arcan. Small pieces of electronically controlled and automated equipment and even the new production lines installed recently are inconspicuous, mingled as they are with Arcan's massive machinery and equipment. The company uniform that usually underscores the difference between Japanese and western companies is not in evidence. As there was no company uniform as such in Arcan, JME did not consider introducing this 'Japanese' custom to its Simcoe Bay plant.

Japanese personnel at the plant, including eight expatriate managers and engineers who are permanently stationed at the plant, are not very visible, being widely dispersed throughout the spacious plant. The Arcan production system has been redesigned by people thoroughly familiar with the production process specific to JME. An army of engineers from Japan were sent through the plant during the setup period. They worked to make the necessary changes to the equipment to fit the configurations of the JME components, and became involved in the training of supervisors and technicians for the new equipment. The company felt the need to keep some of their own Japanese managers and engineers on hand so they could assume overall responsibility for production operation at Simcoe Bay until the plant "got well off the ground." The initial staffing policy was to assign production management and supervision to Canadians, while Japanese expatriate engineers provided consulting and advising. The eight expatriates from the home plant in Japan have remained in the Canadian plant. They occupy such positions as president, manager of finance, marketing manager, coordinator of industrial relations, and production manager. The remaining four are in engineering and technician positions. The president of JME's Canadian plant for the first two years was an engineer with expertise in component manufacturing. As a result he was actively involved in technical and production matters. The current president also has an engineering background, but he is primarily involved in sales, marketing, and broader policy formation, duties which frequently take him away from the factory.

The JME management regards the need for expatriate Japanese managers as temporary. When reorganization has been completed, these positions will be permanently filled by local employees. The corporate strategy of JME is to promote local procurement in their overseas production operations. The Tokyo head office stresses rapid 'localization' of both personnel and procurement. Already the general manager of the plant (vice-president) and the manager of industrial relations as well as several engineers and technicians are new, locally recruited Canadians. The remaining Canadian staff are former Arcan employees.

When Arcan built this plant in 1966, the company was the world leader in electronic component manufacturing. The plant it established was spacious, bright, and clean by Canadian standards, and featured the newest, most advanced, and most capital-intensive equipment. Component manufacturing for visual equipment is a batch production operated on a massive scale. It is highly mechanized with flow-line organization of the production. Everything moves around on conveyors. Parts and components move automatically along tracks from one stage to the next and are rarely handled manually. Component manufacturing is an equipment industry, and the plant requires this large and complex capital-intensive process for its efficient operation.

The size of the factory shocked Japanese personnel when they were exposed to it for the first time. They continue to feel that the plant is too big for its output. In Japan the same level of production would be achieved by a plant "one third this size." For example, there are 7,000 hangers on the conveyor system, each one carrying a product in one stage of production or another. In a compact, more efficient plant, the same work would be done by 2,500 hangers. In other words, one drawback of having a spacious plant is having to carry an extra 4,500 components, more than a day's production, on the work-in-progress. The scarcity of land in Japan has traditionally discouraged over-sized factories as well as waste created by an excessive buildup of inventory (Schonberger, 1982). The American concept and design of space has resulted, in Japanese minds, in the Arcan factory layout which "is insensitive to the operators of the machinery, their convenience or comfort as such" and to the efficiency of the system itself.

JME's management described the plant inherited from Arcan as "a 1966 Ford" which it started altering immediately after the takeover of the business.

> What we see here at the Simcoe Bay plant is the traces of the old Arcan production system. With the existing system alone, without making some changes, we would not have made of this operation a viable business enterprise. No way of us winning or even surviving in the competition in the world market.

The worldwide trend in the component manufacturing industry has been to move toward more and more automation and so-called modernization which results in decreasing an operator's physical input. Instead of manually lifting and carrying items from one stage to another, the main function of the operator is now to inspect the machinery and to check the process so that the whole production process moves smoothly. "A fundamental restructuring" in the technological facilities of the factory thus has to take place, according to

JME management, to fill the twenty-year gap between the production system inherited from Arcan and that of the home plant in Japan.

Altogether, the company agreed to invest $25 million to improve the plant's competitive strength. New equipment and techniques of production have been brought in incrementally. Upgrading the plant facility by providing "the most up-to-date technology and equipment" and other labour-saving techniques has been the top priority of the operation for the past four years. The updating process is going on "almost endlessly." This is not always easy. The installation of one of the major lines of production, described as "the most ambitious project to date," was completed with much difficulty and "unanticipated problems." It took six months for operators to gain enough understanding of and familiarity with the line to ensure its smooth operation. With the completion of the second major production line, however, the improvement in productivity has been considerable: the production level reached the highest ever attained in the plant, and surpassed the Arcan record at its peak. Nevertheless, three years after the onset of plant production, the plant is still regarded as being "in a developmental stage," reducing plant yields. Organizational and procedural changes along with technological updating of lines and equipment continue.

One of the central concerns of this study was with the changes in organizational design which have occurred as a result of the transition from American to Japanese management. The existing literature has not dealt systematically with the process of redesign or its consequences. Instead, it has been suggested that Japanese plants operating overseas, as in the case of auto manufacturers in the United States, have been attempting to replicate almost exactly the hardware technology and production systems of their home country (Shimada and MacDaffie, 1987). It has also been suggested that the Japanese production processes have been replicated with some structural accommodations in response to cultural and environmental differences between Europe and Japan (White and Trevor, 1983).

At Simcoe Bay, JME's organizational restructuring saw three shifts in operation by the fall of 1984. The work force, the administrative staffing, and the production methods were considered to be "about right," and so the plant was "almost ready" to step into full production. How is the "about right" organization redesigned by JME different from the one created by Arcan? What were the ideas and assumptions behind JME's redesign of the organization?

The Organizational Transition from Arcan to JME

The structure adopted by Arcan has been described as "bureaucratic," "the classic plant structure," and "the American corporate structure" by people who were directly involved in the plant operations. In the eyes of the plant's former employees, the internal structure was characterized by a configuration of design parameters which Mintzberg (1979) terms the Machine Bureaucracy: there were precise definitions of duties, responsibilities and power, and a well-developed hierarchy. The organization was highly formalized, and decision-making was centralized at the U.S. headquarters. A worker with ten years service with Arcan describes the structure as he saw it:

> Arcan had a structure, the same one everywhere in the American plants. For instance, in QC Department, under the departmental manager, there were three managers, and under them three foremen, technicians, and hourly-rated inspectors. This structure and the reporting relationships between the people were exactly the same everywhere. It was the American-type bureaucratic structure. Management in Simcoe Bay went by that structure. Whether it was necessary or not, it didn't matter. The plant was fairly well managed from the States.

Figure 1 depicts Arcan's structure in December, 1981, shortly before the decision was made to close the plant. The structure was created by the divisional headquarters, and was uniformly applied from plant to plant and passed on to Simcoe Bay. There were approximately 200 individuals who occupied salaried positions and 700 hourly workers. This structure was established in the early 1970s as the plant grew to full capacity production with three shifts, and was sustained with few major changes throughout the years. (See Figure 3.1)

The Arcan organization chart can be contrasted with two JME charts: for spring, 1985 (Figure 3.2), a year and a half after the company opened the Canadian plant, and for June, 1986 (Figure 3.3). In 1985 there were sixty-five

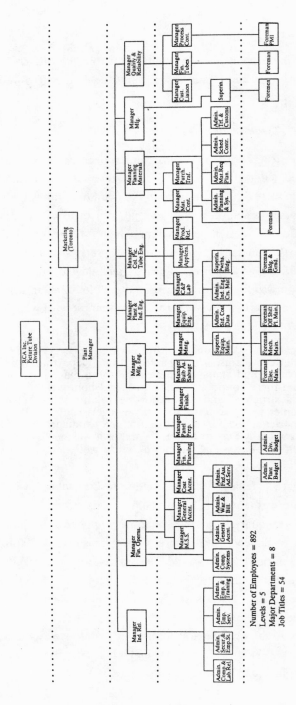

Figure 3.1: ORGANIZATION CHART – Arcan December 1981

Number of Employees = 892
Levels = 5
Major Departments = 8
Job Titles = 54

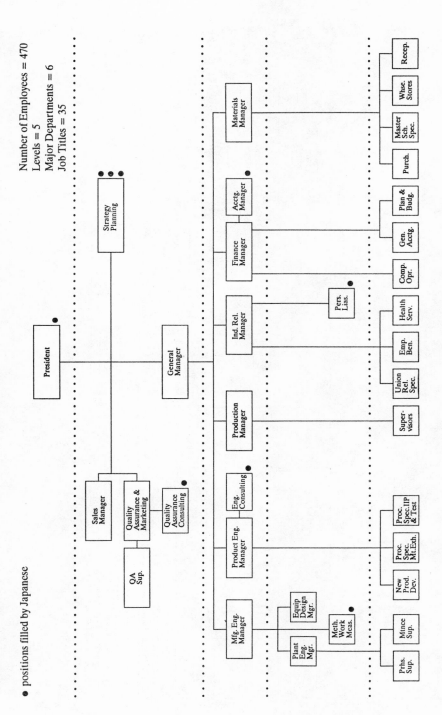

• positions filled by Japanese

Number of Employees = 470
Levels = 5
Major Departments = 6
Job Titles = 35

Figure 3.2: ORGANIZATION CHART – JME March 1985

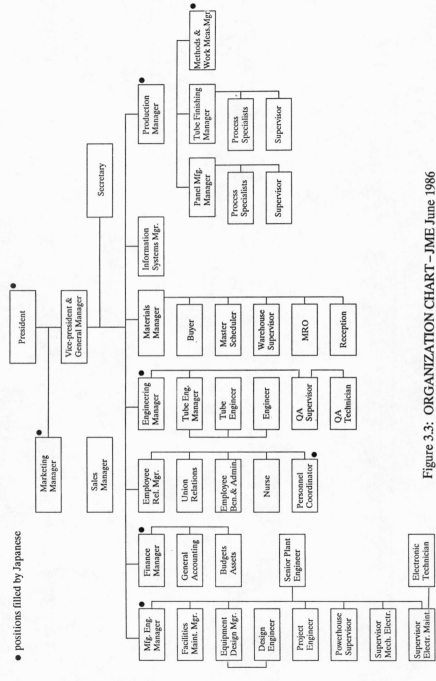

Figure 3.3: ORGANIZATION CHART – JME June 1986

● positions filled by Japanese

salaried workers. A year later there were seventy-five. These numbers were about one-third the number employed by Arcan. The number of production workers, about 400, remained unchanged over this period.

The figures indicate that both plants had five levels in their hierarchy. The number of jobs existing laterally across the Arcan organization was fifty-four, in contrast to the thirty-eight job titles for JME (including the positions currently filled by the eight Japanese expatriates on short-term assignment). Within the Arcan structure eight functionally specialized departments existed while JME has so far established only six. The quality control and reliability assurance department was eliminated; Arcan's three engineering-related departments were reduced to two by JME. At the same time JME has given its Canadian plant two additional functions to perform which did not exist under Arcan: strategic planning and marketing (Figure 3.2).

In the initial, rather tentative organizational design created by JME, the two activities of planning and marketing belonged to the top management area, and did not exist as independent, separate departments. Later, the three Japanese expatriate managers assigned to strategic planning were reassigned to other engineering positions, and the planning activities were incorporated into the domain of the president's office.

Although these two activities were only gradually integrated into the Simcoe Bay plant hierarchy, JME's organization charts suggest that strategic planning, as well as marketing strategy, are now done at the Canadian plant and not at company headquarters. Arcan depended largely on the divisional head office in the United States and the Canadian head office for its marketing and planning. In fact, under Arcan management, as the chart indicates, the Simcoe Bay plant was not responsible for product development or overall market strategy. JME's Canadian plant, on the other hand, is expected to "stand on [its] own feet technically" and to "do a lot of its own market research and design development," because firstly, headquarters are far away, and secondly, they "know only so much about the North American market and its customers." The JME charts indicate that the degree of "truncation" in the Canadian plant has been reduced due to the change in ownership. The issue of truncation in foreign-owned firms is important as it measures the degree of control exercised by the parent company and of dependency on the subsidiary, and thus will be taken up for further discussion in another section of this report.

Next, the most obvious difference between the organization charts is the size of the administrative staff. Arcan had an elaborate administrative structure with a large percentage of personnel not engaged in production activities. JME has reduced the administrative staff by one-third by eliminating the managerial-specialist positions in the middle level. JME started with only four 'middle' managers stationed in the engineering area while Arcan had thirty-four jobs at this level filled by either managers, administrators, or superintendents in manufacturing (Figures 3.1 and 3.2). In the past year, the number of JME middle managers has been increased to eight as a result of the two newly created positions in the production and engineering areas respectively (Figure 3.3). Still, the gap of staffing at this level in the two organizations remains wide and significant. The organizational changes were described by two employees, a supervisor in plant maintenance and a machine operator on the shop floor:

> The biggest difference is the decrease in the salaried or non-production workers. The QC people, for example, no longer exist with JME. The job I am doing now (supervisor in plant maintenance) was done by four people before, and now I am the only one. If there were four technicians with Arcan, there are one or two technicians now. The same thing applies in the manufacturing.

> JME does not want to lay off people, once they are hired. They are struggling through with less people, which is harder on some of the workers. Arcan's biggest down-fall was the number of people. They had a lot of extra people to make sure the job got done. Arcan had a crew of twenty-two janitors. Now we have only four. They used to keep the floor spotless. Now it's dirty.

The JME management intended to create the "leanest possible structure" and to form their staffing and manpower policies based on that structure. The head office in Tokyo exercised a fair amount of control in setting the staffing policy and in establishing employment levels for various departments. Upon purchasing the plant, the company had made an agreement with the government "to create and maintain a regular work force consisting of about 500 employees." In component manufacturing the economy of scale is a critical factor, and the minimum scale in the case of the Simcoe Bay plant is considered to be "no less than 1.5 million components a year." A work force of 500 employees was thus calculated on the basis of the ratio between output and number of employees, and considered to be optimum given the production capacity of the plant.[1] The management's responsibility is thus to keep expanding and modernizing "without firing any of the workers" already hired to achieve full utilization of the plant and its human resources.

From the outset the management were determined, maintains the plant manager, "to constantly pursue efficiency," and this determination made JME take aggressive measures to cut manpower budgets substantially by not expanding the staff size of the organization. The result is a broad-based structure with fewer higher positions and staff specialists, as evidenced in the company's organizational charts.

The ideas behind the organizational structure may have been derived from the Japanese style of 'adversity management' which cannot tolerate the excessive cost of non-productive staff and specialists any more than it can tolerate inventory buildups. In the Japanese view, the central players in manufacturing organizations are the line – the production supervisors and the workers. These are the productive people. Thus, they must be experts. In Japan workers control a good portion of the machinery and equipment; they set it up, run it, and maintain it, thus requiring less coordination. Because of the diversity of tasks they perform, line people are given continuous training and education. The jobs, both of workers and managers, are rotated systematically, so that workers will have a broad familiarity with the tasks associated with the entire production process and managers will have a broad perspective enabling them to make major decisions. Staff, on the other hand, including maintenance workers on the shop floor, are considered extras; they are needed only if and when the line people request their services. In addition, they support the line but not the management. The fewer the number of staff members and specialists, the more efficient operations become. In his comparison of Japanese and Western manufacturing techniques, Schonberger (1982:197) is critical of the "wastefulness of staff growth and over specialization" in Western industry:

> In the 1950's, it [Western industry] prospered and ate fatty goods, and now it is suffering from hardening of the arteries. The fat is nonproductive staff, which not only is expensive but actually is an obstacle to fast response and the pursuit of actions done for the good of the whole organization.

"The Western penchant of specialization" is a serious problem, maintains Schonberger, because it makes the system of job rotation difficult to operate. This prevents specialists from ever acquiring a broad, company-wide outlook. As a result, coordination costs dramatically increase.

Arcan seemed to suffer from this Western penchant. As the company grew in the postwar decades, it added more and more services, created new staff units, and sought increasingly to bring in support staff and specialists. The structure based on this expansionist ideology was transferred to the Canadian plant from the parent company, and sustained until the recession of the early 1980s. "The number of people" or "the heavy staffing" both in production and non-production areas was undoubtedly a problem in Arcan, according to the comments of many informants during the field work and during the interviews with ex-Arcan employees. The plant manager of JME earlier commented that:

> We are running a very lean kind of organization with only sixty-five salaried people against Arcan's 215. Surely something has to go. The biggest difference right now is the attitude of the people. The attitude of the salaried people is changing finally after two years of the operation. They've come to accept the fact that this business can be run with 65 people. It doesn't need 200 people to run it.

JME has transformed an over-specialized company into more a Japanese-style organization in which line managers and supervisors have a full measure of responsibility for their department's performance. With a broad base and with fewer staff specialists, the JME supervisor-to-worker ratio has become a high one. The JME factory has one supervisor for every twenty-two workers on average, the size of the work unit being twelve. Some supervisors have more than one unit to work with. At Arcan there was one foreman for every twenty-five to thirty workers, according to a former superintendent in manufacturing. White and Trevor (1983:35) likewise note that the supervisor-manager ratio in the Japanese-owned firm they studied was high, eighteen per cent. This is twice as great a proportion as was observed in other British firms. In the engineering industry as a whole, according to the information from the British source cited by White and Trevor, the proportion of managers and supervisors to workers is no more than twelve per cent. The 'Japanese tendency' towards putting more emphasis on the line function than on the staff function is reflected in this higher ratio elsewhere as well.

The line positions, the first supervisory jobs, are staffed generously, but no provision of other support for manufacturing activities is provided. Eliminating Arcan's middle supervisory position of superintendents, JME has only one supervisory category, people called supervisors. The function of the supervisor and the scope of his/her authority have been widened.

Mintzberg (1979) argues that variations in the unit size can account in part for differences in the mechanisms used to coordinate work. Where unit size is larger, the work is highly standardized. Arcan's greater span of control suggests that the company relied extensively on standardization of work processes to facilitate coordination. With the elaborate systems of standardization designed by the heavily staffed techno-structure, the Arcan supervisor spent less time on direct supervision of each worker, thus allowing a greater number of employees to report to him. (In the front section there were units consisting of seventy to eighty operators under one foremanship.)

The lower span of control in JME, on the other hand, reflects less vertical and horizontal specialization of production tasks and a broader role assigned to the supervisors. Coordination in a unit is achieved through mutual adjustment and direct supervision. Being a leader of the work team, the JME supervisor has to supervise the unit's activities more closely, monitor quality control activities, and be more readily available for consultation and advice. The changing role of supervisors will be discussed more fully in a later section of this report.

Organizational restructuring has indeed been drastic, the management admits, as the reduction (or the shortage) of personnel has affected everybody involved in the operation "directly and personally." In some areas the plant is understaffed. The production manager sees, for instance, the need for personnel who would coordinate all the production activities throughout the shifts. The measures taken have nonetheless been effective and have been "a good thing," according to him, because they have acted as "shock treatment" to make people realize that "change was inevitable and absolutely necessary." Management's goal has been accomplished; "people's awareness has been provoked if not changed."

> We have to make further changes in organizational structure and staffing. As a basic principle, however, we would stick to the original ideas – to keep this organization as lean and small as possible. We'll try to run this factory with a smaller number of people. Additional people will be put into areas only when a high level of value added is anticipated.

Changes in Priorities

One way of making a comparison in the Arcan and JME plant with respect to structure is to examine the differences in the priority attached to functional activities. The Aston Specialization Scale is a useful tool for comparing the priorities of the two companies. The scale lists sixteen different functional activities, such as production control, accounting, maintenance, and market research, which are present in many manufacturing organizations (Pugh, Hickson, Hinings, and Turner, 1968). Table 3.1 compares the activities given the highest priority by both JME and Arcan.

Table 3.1: Top Five Functional Activities Endorsed*

Arcan	JME
Inspection (quality Control)	Customer Service
Maintenance	Methods
Production Control	Design and Development
Design and Development	Production Control
Employment	Employment

*The endorsement was done by the plant manager of JME for JME, and for Arcan by the three ex-Arcan managers. All were asked to choose five functions or activities emphasized most importantly within the respective organization and were further asked to rank the five of the 16 items from one to five in order of importance.

The plant manager of JME emphasized that customer service is the area most vigorously pursued by JME from the strategic marketing point of view:

> Each customer's request is slightly different from the others. To satisfy the specific needs of the customer is our marketing policy and our mandate right now. The complaints from the customer or problems have to be looked into immediately without delay.

The company tries to optimize the designs of components to meet the customer's technical requirements. The Simcoe Bay plant produces multiple types and sizes of components, unlike Arcan which tended to sell one type of component produced in two sizes at the Simcoe Bay plant. JME's insistence on product mix and on variation within lines reduces productivity and raises cost by requiring extra labour, thus placing the company at a disadvantage. Nonetheless, it is "required rather than optional" from the point of view of JME's marketing strategy. The plant is in direct contact with customers on a daily basis. Responding to problems regarding the products promptly, and finding immediate remedies for these problems are given top priority by JME. The plant manager claims that this has become part of the routine in the daily operations.

At Arcan, on the other hand, the most important functional activity was inspection rather than customer service according to ex-Arcan managers.

> I would say that as far as quality control was concerned, tremendous emphasis was put on it in our organization. That was always number one and we always said, 'Concentrate on the quality and the number will automatically come.' There was inspection throughout the whole process. There was 100% inspection at the end. The amount of money we spent on testing was incredible. We overtested. We really did.

> Quality control inspection was very important and the quality was well-controlled at Arcan. A lot of people [in fact 20-25 staff members alone] were employed in the Quality Control Department doing nothing but inspection. That was a big job for Arcan.

Responsibility for quality was assumed by specialist staff inspectors rather than by production operators. Finished products were taken to a quality-testing room away from the shop floor, and "checking and double checking" was thoroughly undertaken to ensure that sub-standard products were seldom permitted to "slip through." The concern with the quality of the products at Arcan, in fact, was regarded as its greatest strength by people involved in the operation.

> We made damn good components.

> The components made in Simcoe Bay were the best in the country. Customers asked for them.

> The quality was well controlled. The Simcoe Bay plant was, quality-wise, the best factory with the lower scrap rate.

JME, by contrast, introduced to its Canadian plant the method most commonly used by Japanese companies. The responsibility for quality is placed in the hands of the production department and quality checking is built into operators' jobs. The basic idea is that quality begins with production, that it is "everyone's problem," and that it requires company-wide "habits of improvement." A worker in close contact with a supervisor is expected to take a large measure of responsibility for improving the quality of products.

JME management, therefore, had no intention of creating a QC department as such, separate from production – another reflection of their determination to keep the support structure as lean as possible. In fact, a useful comparison can be made between the differences in the factory structure created at Simcoe Bay by Arcan and JME, and those studied by Cusumano (1985:329) in his discussion of auto assembly plants in the United States and Japan. The average American assembly plant, according to the data cited by Cusumano (Table 3.2) has 2.3 times more workers assigned to quality control (including inspection) and to other functional areas than do Japanese factories. Japanese workers not only conduct their own quality control and inspections, as figures in the table further indicate, but they also do considerable maintenance and janitorial and other work. These additional functions performed by Japanese workers, Cusumano argues, have

Table 3.2: **Assembly Plant Comparison: Japan-United States, ca. 1980** (employees)

Function	Japan	United States	Ratio Japan = 1.0
Quality Control	156	359	2.3
(inspection)	(120)	(302)	(2.5)
(emissions)	(26)	(37)	(1.4)
(emgineering)	(10)	(20)	(2.0)
Production Control	95	310	3.3
(scheduling)	(11)	(66)	(6.0)
(materials)	(56)	(216)	(3.9)
Product Engineering	22	6	0.3
Manufacturing Engineering	132	411	3.1
(maintenance)	(62)	(207)	(3.3)
(janitors)	(10)	(114)	(11.4)
Production	1324	2640	2.0
(painting)	(250)	(421)	(1.7)
(assembly)	(641)	(1603)	(2.5)
Management Staff	33	132	4.0
Grand Total	1762	3885*	2.2
Hours Per Small Car	14	31	2.2

Cited From: Cusmano, M., *The Japanese Automobile Industry*. p. 329

* Total includes 27 union officials

Figures in parenthesis are examples of subcategories and do not always equal the totals for the individual major functions.

reduced overall personnel levels in assembly, supervision, production scheduling, and material control to less than half of those in comparable American plants. The difference between the two organizations in the manner in which quality control is organized at Simcoe Bay is important because quality management affects the structure and climate of the total organization. This issue will be examined in detail later in a separate chapter.

The management under Arcan and JME also differed, though less markedly, in the priority given to other functional activities. JME's management believes that "just to remain competitive," it must surpass the efficiency levels not only of Arcan's former operation, but of their other competitors as well. In order to do so it must continue to improve quality levels and manufacturing methods. For this reason manufacturing methods, design and development and production control, all of them related manufacturing activities, are given a very high priority by JME and are rated just below customer service in their list of crucial functional activities (See Table 3.1).

> The constant pursuit of efficiency is our way of doing things here. Everything is geared toward attaining this goal. Everybody is supposed to work towards the goal of becoming more efficient. Each report and communication has a yield or efficiency measurement.

Production control is important, but JME does not depend on computers as decision-making instruments. There is only one specialist assigned responsibility for operating the computer system for the entire organization. Decisions are made by people, relying heavily on their common sense. Thus, production scheduling, for instance, is "virtually a manual operation."

In the Arcan plant, production-related activities, maintenance, and production control in particular were high on their list of priorities, and were given slightly higher priority than under JME (Table 3.1). As with JME, design and development were also viewed as very important functions with about thirty specialists and staff engineers engaged therein.

The two organizations under investigation have proven to differ substantially in terms of their major design parameters and their consequent staffing and manpower policies. The differences are the results of a partial transition from a mechanistic to an organic structure of organization. JME gives great weight to flexibility and adaptability. Its organization tends to adopt an organic, less formalized internal structure. The plant structure under Arcan management, on the other hand, tended to be characterized by a set of mechanistic design features. It was formalized. The management employed rules, procedures, and a clear hierarchy of authority extensively. The organization was also centralized, with most decisions being made at the top. Nonetheless, it was, as some informants described it, a "neatly organized" plant. The transition from a mechanistic to an organic structure and the dramatic reductions in personnel have been accompanied by significant changes in the definition of the roles of supervisors, technicians and hourly workers. These changes will be the topic of the examination and will be discussed in the following chapters.

38

Note

1. JME's head office estimated that with a regular work force of 500 the target number of products to be manufactured at their Canadian plant would be somewhere between 1.5 million and 2 million components a year, or 2,500 units per worker. At their home plant in Japan, approximately 1,000 employees are engaged in components manufacturing. This figure includes some part-timers and casual and contract workers. With this work force the Japanese plant has been making about 4 million units a year in the past few years. How fast the Canadian plant can attain the level of production and productivity of their home plant, head office claims, will be dependent on the introduction of new automated equipment and other labour-saving techniques.

Chapter Four
Redesigning the Job Structure

The Simcoe Bay plant, like the component manufacturing industry within which it operates, epitomizes mass production. At least seventy per cent of its employees are regarded as mass producers; their jobs are simplified to the point that almost anyone, once trained, can perform the tasks of other employees. In the front section of the plant jobs tend to be physically lighter, less demanding, and here female employees predominate, while the jobs in the back end involve some heavy lifting, are more physically demanding and are usually held by men. Nonetheless, jobs within these two broadly divided operations at the plant are generally transferable; many employees are capable of moving to another section within each of the operations. Most of the jobs in this plant, as in other plants using "long-linked technology," are standardized and repetitive (Thompson, 1967), and considered semi-skilled. Workers are secure in the knowledge that basically the same things are required day after day; at the same time they are often bored by the repetition.

The way Arcan had its jobs structured at its Simcoe Bay plant seems, judging from the pieces of information obtained from former employees on the shop floor, to have been similar to the one depicted in the literature dealing with manufacturing enterprises (Doeringer and Piore, 1971; Grinker, et al., 1970). The job structure was divided into functional departments, and at the production level alone fourteen large classifications involving various levels of skills were established. Within a classification jobs were further grouped into grades, and wage rates were assigned to these grades. Jobs were nonetheless largely homogeneous in their content, although some work stations required more skill and knowledge than others. The differences between them were both small and incremental, one of the characteristic features of the job structure noted commonly in North American manufacturing enterprises by researchers in the field (Grinker, et al. 1970 49). At Arcan certain workers were rewarded with a five or ten cents an hour premium for slightly more skilled tasks, but the spread between top and bottom in the work force was rather small, so that it could not be considered upgrading in the sense that a worker moves into a job requiring greater skill and experience, getting paid more money. The labour contract effective in 1981, the last year of the Arcan operation, documented that the wages at Arcan ranged from $5.87 for a janitor II to $8.32 for a tradesman, the average being $7.00. Wages were differentiated into twenty-nine rates equal to the number of the identified jobs, a differentiation that had accumulated over the years of the plant operation. These wage distinctions tended to fragment worker interests and served as a motivational force. Workers were promoted through a sequence of jobs forming a job ladder designed to give workers a sense of upward movement; the larger the number of wage rates, the wider the opportunity to move ahead, at least in the worker's perception.

Informal on-the-job training, largely prevalent for blue-collar manufacturing jobs (Doeringer and Piore), was the only training provided at Arcan. In the West relatively greater emphasis has been placed, in theory at least, on the role of general training, as compared to specific on-the-job training in the formation of workers' skills. In practice, however, Doeringer and Piore pointed out, based on evidence from their research, as enterprise specificity of skills is increased in an "internal labour market" where most workers are involved in North America, on-the-job training has increasingly been resorted to as a means of training. Thus, firm-specific, on-the-job training is no longer a feature unique to the Japanese type of labour market. Customs and rules of work contribute to the formation and transmission of firm-specific skills. At Arcan, on-the-job training was most often informally conducted during working hours by foremen, and not recognized as a distinct process at all. It was simply assumed that a worker who had been around for a while would know how to do certain things. For relatively simple operating jobs, new workers were typically given no more than a brief job demonstration.

At the semi-skilled level a mobility pattern would usually involve a move from an operator to a QC inspector, machine attendant, repairman or relief man within the same department. In addition to the higher pay, these jobs offered a variety of activities not accorded to line operators who comprised the majority of workers. While such higher-rated jobs were normally filled by workers in the lesser-skilled classifications when a vacancy arose, in practice this was not a continuous progression. There was almost no internal movement out of the semi-skilled classifications to the highest skill levels. Such openings were relatively rare.

When an opening occurred in a department, notice was posted and an employee was expected to apply for the job within three days, stating his/her qualifications for the vacancy. There would likely be several people in the job class immediately below the vacant one, and if all bid, the more senior would get it. Seniority was, therefore, almost the sole criterion for moving incrementally within the operators' ranks. A few exceptions were those rare cases in which management could prove the lack of ability or fitness of a candidate. Job progressions, however small they might be, were automatically available to the junior workers if they stayed around long enough. The rules of seniority simplified the selection process since no serious disputes could arise from promoting the more senior worker. For this reason they were persistently adhered to not only for job assignments but also for promotions and layoffs by both the union and the workers in general.

With the coming of the new owner together with its new top management, what has happened to the Arcan job structure? What changes have actually taken place in the content and method of jobs and tasks workers perform daily? Several questions relating to changes in job structure were included in the questionnaire which we distributed to plant employees. In response to an open-ended question dealing with changes in general, a fair number of respondents simply said that they saw "no difference," while a few elaborated somewhat:

I don't find much difference, because I'm doing much the same job for both companies.

I don't find the work I'm doing now any different, except I've a lot more responsibility.

Only the automation has changed things.

Job rotation is the only thing that is different.

Very little difference in the way the actual work is done.

Basically the same but Arcan was better organized.

No difference. Factory work is factory work, whoever the employer is.

In contrast to the "no difference" response, other respondents mentioned that they had "more responsibility," "more workload," and in addition that the content of the job had changed:

JME expects you to do 3 or 4 jobs. Impossible to do one well while trying to do 3 or 4.

With Arcan, engineers did the engineering work. Now workers are expected to do jobs that engineers used to do.

Employees were not formed to do janitorial services. Now they are.

With Arcan, management told you what, when, and how to do; you didn't do anything which wasn't your job.

Now you are on your own too much. Workers are being relied on to give information concerning problems with product.

Arcan's point of view was that nobody knows their job better than the person doing their job.

Now the worker has a little more responsibility and is allowed to move from job to job.

We maintain our own machines instead of waiting for a machine attendant for minor changes or repairs.

It is not boring with JME because you haven't got time to be bored. Learning more. More dependent on workers. Minimum supervision. You really have to know your job.

More initiative to do your own work.

> With Arcan you had a job to do. With this place several jobs to do and they want them done immediately. I'm doing more than one job because the line was redesigned.

> I've learned a lot more than I did with Arcan. More detail on how the machinery works. At Arcan it was just there's your job and you didn't know another job. You just knew the one you were on. You're learning more now.

> They are now so understaffed that they put people anywhere. I come into work tonight. I don't know where I'm going to be. I have a specific job I am supposed to do if they leave me there. They just use you all over the place.

The answers to another set of questions asked in the questionnaire supplement the complex views and feelings expressed in the above quotations. In assessing the differences as they experienced them in performing their jobs on the shop floor, twenty-one per cent of the respondents who were ex-Arcan employees answered that their influence had increased, sixty-four per cent agreed that their responsibility had increased, eighty-six per cent that their workload had increased, and seventy-two per cent that their jobs had become more stressful. Thus, the very large majority of ex-Arcan employees claimed that their workload and the consequent work pressure have increased. People in interviews almost always connected tightness of staffing levels with broader responsibilities, and pointed out, for example, that under the new management inspection of the quality of products was now assigned to operators. People do in fact have more than one job to perform now, not because jobs are rotated systematically, but because under the manning policy of the new management operators are required to be flexibly stationed when and if the production schedule requires this. "Uncertainty about where you're going to be when you come into work is stressful," said one male worker, an indication of the stress experienced by seven out of ten respondents in our survey as the above-mentioned figure suggests.

JME's initial negotiations with the union upon taking over the plant from Arcan in 1983 centered on three crucial issues: 1) gaining acceptance of a single job classification within operators' ranks to replace the existing fourteen classifications; 2) rotating jobs among operators as well as among skilled workers and technicians; and 3) getting rid of rules of seniority as a primary determinant in layoffs, job assignments and promotion. However, these proposals were soon withdrawn from the agenda of the negotiation as being "too drastic" or "unrealistic" for the would-be employees, the majority of whom were to be recalled ex-Arcan employees. Instead a compromise was sought between the parties involved in the transformation of the business, and the new company agreed in the end to accept the overall organization of human resources and the job structure already established with Arcan.

The JME approach to the organization of human resources, in short, has since been a piecemeal one. The company managed to broaden the job classifications by differentiating six levels of skill at the operator's level, thus making it more like the Japanese system, and the classification scheme has remained unchanged since. Jobs under the current contract, however, are largely like the ones with Arcan; they have merely been streamlined from twenty-nine to twenty-one categories which are linked to twenty-one different wage rates. The compromise reached between management and the union has had a number of troubling consequences and has led to considerable dissatisfaction on both sides, as the following discussion of each of the three crucial issues pinpointed by JME negotiators will make clear.

Job Classification and Rotation

As we have seen, JME initially negotiated with the union to gain acceptance of a single job classification, rather than, as they could have, shifting the basis of compensation from the heaviness of the work to the variety of pieces of machinery and equipment an employee can operate, or to the employee's understanding of the production process. Arcan's system of functionally based job classification had linked wages to the physical demand of work and only secondarily to the skill required. Because of the centrality of heaviness of work to the classification system, women workers, comprising about forty per cent of the work force, were and still are heavily concentrated in the lowest paid classifications. Despite the fact that multi-skilling can increase flexibility in staffing and in organizational structure, the concept was never encouraged by the Arcan system. Koike (1984: 66-67), in his discussion on skill formation systems in the U.S. and Japan, pointed to the difference in the range of mobility among workers on the shop floor as "the most noteworthy difference" between the two. In Japanese firms, stated Koike, "regular workers tend to move from one position to another regularly or irregularly, ultimately to experience almost all positions in the workshop."

At JME greater emphasis on a number of skills and on a degree of mastery might have encouraged employees to upgrade their skills, and might have increased acceptance of job rotation as a means of achieving increasingly worthy work. Instead of seeking a single job classification, JME might have done better to adopt a compensation system rewarding multi-skilling and encouraging upgrading as done by Japanese companies elsewhere (White and Trevor, 1983). Such an approach would at least have encouraged employees to move among tasks rather than specializing in one. In addition, if compensation was to be based not only on a mastery of individual skills but also on one's depth of understanding of the production process, then it would be clearer to employees that thinking as well as doing was expected of operators and that a holistic perspective on the production process was required. Since job rotation is one of the ways of acquiring such a perspective, this system of compensation might well have led to a clear association on the part of both supervisors and operators between job rotation and systematically increased employee access to increasingly worthy work.

North Americans are prone to view job rotation among production workers merely as a strategy for reducing employee boredom and alienation. Such rotation is understood to increase the number and variety of standardized and formalized tasks workers perform thus increasing the breadth of their job. However, job rotation can also be seen as a form of organization essential to the development of flexible structures; as such it is widely practised, for instance, in manufacturing plants in Japan (Monden, 1983; Cole, 1979; Shimada and MacDuffie, 1987; Koike; 1984). Rotation permits the development of multi-skilling; it encourages a responsiveness to others within the organization which generates an appreciation of the need for mutual adjustment, and it provides an in-depth understanding of the production processes and of the flows comprising the existing organization of those processes. In this view, job rotation involves those engaged in production in continually developing, evaluating and refining the structure of production processes. This involvement leads to an increase in both the breadth and depth of the operator's work. Operators acquire more information and have more opportunities for using that information to increase the productivity of the organization employing them. Through such opportunities, operators are better able both to develop and to use manual and thinking skills, increasing the worthiness of the work they do.

JME sought to introduce plant-wide job rotation at the outset of their operation at Simcoe Bay. The plant manager explains their reasoning:

> We thought that people would have welcomed a kind of training program of job rotation to broaden the scope of their work so that they could do many, many jobs in the factory instead of doing just one. We thought there would be solid cooperation from the workers. That wasn't the case. They seem more comfortable in a routine task. If you ask them to change their thinking and do different tasks, there are all kinds of reasons and excuses why they can't.

This remark suggests that JME would have liked to emphasize multi-skilling and greater breadth in jobs; whereas workers preferred narrow to broad jobs and, thus, resisted a wider range of mobility. However, the plant manager's argument that job rotation constitutes a training program fails to make explicit exactly what skills JME hoped that job rotation would develop. Was the worker merely to be trained to perform more than one standardized task, or was he/she also being trained to operate in a flexible organization? The emphasis placed by the plant manager on job rotation as a technique for changing workers' thinking suggests that the other functions associated with using job rotation to facilitate a more flexible organization constituted an implicit rather than an explicit objective on the part of JME. This objective was never adequately explained to the workers.

The president of the union explained the reaction of some workers on the shop floor to the proposed policies on job rotation:

> JME tried job rotation, but it never worked. We [the union executives] thought it would never work. People are not used to rotating their jobs here. Most people like to do the same job, even though it is repetitive. We've a lot of older people who are afraid of learning something new. They like to feel, when they come in to work, they know what they are going to do. Knowing that they are not learning something new every day, and they are not nervous with it, people feel more secure.

Interviews with union officials, supervisors and workers indicate that when initially introduced job rotation was not viewed by employees as a training program, and the advantages and disadvantages of greater breadth were not widely agreed upon. These supervisors' comments reflect this view:

> There are good points and bad points to job rotation. Some employees want to do one job, one job only. There are other employees who want to do different jobs every day. Job rotation works for some but it doesn't work for all. Some people have the mentality to be able to rotate. Some people have a long concentration span on repeating.... We basically had to stop job rotation because some people just can't do it.

These perspectives were reinforced by answers to a question given in our questionnaire. Sixty-one per cent of the employees who responded to the questions on job rotation felt that "job rotation makes work more interesting," while thirty-one per cent agreed that "job rotation reduces my ability to do the job right," thirty-two per cent that "job rotation leaves me unsure of what to expect," and about fifteen per cent that "job rotation increases my workload." The large majority of employees thus agreed that job rotation makes works more interesting while slightly less than a third of them opposed the idea of job rotation, being uncomfortable with the uncertainty which could be caused by rotating. Only about fifteen per cent believed it would increase their workload.

In the in-depth interviews some workers stressed the contribution of job rotation to reducing monotony by increasing the variety of work.

> I like job rotation... because you're not stuck in one spot doing one monotonous thing over and over like we were.... I like the job rotation because you're doing something different every other day....We're on the same station for two days and then we rotate, and it makes it a lot better because the job is not quite so boring.

> A good job is one where everything you do is different. Everything has to be handled different. Makes you think.

> I personally prefer to rotate jobs. Definitely boring a lot of it. When you rotate you don't get quite as bored with your job....We don't have high education, but we're not stupid either. A lot of the guys on the floor are a lot smarter than the supervisors. They know a lot more.

> There are six different jobs in our department. It's the same thing but one day I may be doing more of this and less of that so I find it better. Job rotation for me is the best.

Other workers, however, viewed job rotation as undermining their ability to be as productive as possible and their ability to perform standardized tasks without errors.

> If you want to go to another job, you should apply for it. I don't think you should be bounced from one job to the next. You can't get training. They put you on a job for three or four hours. They show you the basics, but you can't learn a job like testing in eight hours.

> Anybody specializing in a job would do a heck of a lot better job. You're doing the same job every day. If you like it, you don't get bored. If I don't like it, I could put in for a transfer.

These workers argued that job rotation reduces responsibility and undermines quality. Their assumption is that employees define the task to be performed as standardized and formalized; speed and the number of errors made define how well they are doing. These employees do not see themselves as having responsibility for developing, evaluating or refining proposals for improving the way the production processes are organized. Instead, it seems obvious, they define themselves as doing rather than thinking, as operating in a bureaucratic rather than flexible structure.

In any case, at JME, systematic, plant-wide job rotation was abandoned by management at an early stage, and left to the discretion of the supervisor. One supervisor explains his use of it as follows:

> I think there should be some rotation, but not the way we were doing it in the beginning. Within my shift, we switch among different jobs every day. The differences are very small so we can do it. There seems no one best way to deal with change.

This supervisor is clearly not emphasizing multi-skilling. He merely rotates employees among pieces of machinery located within the same work station which are only slightly differentiated from one another.

The system of job rotation that JME introduced was a technique for dealing with boredom and fatigue in part, replacing the "half-on, half-off" practice. Yet the plant-wide rotation has been abondoned due to pressure from supervisors and workers. It will take some time for both the union and management to work out mutually acceptable criteria other than seniority for assigning jobs and promotion. Doringer and Piore (1971; 26) argued that some procedures, such as considering seniority in promotion and layoffs, can become so embedded in custom outside the plant that they are exceedingly difficult to change. It seems doubtful that the crucial aspects of Japanese management, as depicted by Shimada and MacDuffie, will ever be implemented in JME's Canadian plant.

Employees thus move from one standardized, formalized job to another closely related job. As a result, job rotation is not expected to contribute in any substantial way to the development of flexible structures.

Indeed, supervisors seemed to view job rotation largely as a technique for reducing boredom and increasing individual motivation:

> We still try to rotate jobs....Quality-wise, productivity-wise, I know it's better if they are happy with what they are doing...if they like a particular job, that's fine with me. They can stay and retire with it. Those people who like to rotate, I will try to rotate them. I don't see why we cannot do that.

> I rotate people between two positions regularly. They like it. They don't get bored by shifting the jobs. Rotation between departments is impossible because you have to stay with the job classification. That is the union's rule. I think my people would even take rotation between departments well. They like to rotate around.

These statements suggest that the North American perspective on job rotation prevails perhaps more persistently among supervisors than workers, and that they do not assess job rotation in terms of the contribution it can make to the development of flexible structures. Supervisors do not recognize that restricting the use of job rotation makes it increasingly difficult for operators and for themselves to make the transition from a closed to an open system perspective, from coordinating by rules and behaviour formalization to mutual adjustment, and from following directions to responding to others.

Because job rotation is viewed by supervisors only as motivating workers and not as facilitating the transition to flexible structures, too little attention has been devoted to ensuring its adoption. This failure to understand the theory behind the notion of rotating jobs on the part of supervisors, coupled with the fairly strong resistance shown by some workers, made the Japanese management realize the difficulty and confusion in implementing the system as originally envisioned at their Canadian plant. For that reason job rotation at JME became optional, and its use has been limited up to now. It has been used primarily to achieve absentee relief and rotation among closely related jobs within a single work station. It has not been used explicitly to provide workers with a greater understanding of the interdependencies within the plant so that workers would realize "the impact of their job on the rest of the system."

If job rotation is to promote a growing understanding of the production processes and the way they are organized, workers must rotate among differentiated jobs; as one worker commented, "just moving among machines has no effect since the set-up is all the same." Job rotation becomes an educational and useful process for skill formation only when the organization of the manufacturing process is flexible rather than fixed. Cole's elaborate discussion and analysis on work redesign which focuses on a Japanese auto body plant (Cole, 1979: ch. VI), as a case study, provides the details of the educational process that the plant as a whole went through. Rotating is thus an ongoing process, as is education. It is the flexibility of the process which provides opportunities to think, to identify distinct contingencies affecting the appropriate course of action.

On the basis of our data, we can conclude that the limited job rotation which JME attempted to introduce at Simcoe Bay has not facilitated the transition from bureaucratic to flexible structures. Because it was not pursued vigorously, and because no adequate reorientation was provided, it has not resulted in implementing the skill formation system that JME management initially planned, nor has it promoted a transition from behaviour formalization to mutual adjustment. Likewise, it has not encouraged employees to recognize that JME's internal structure, unlike Arcan's, should be perpetually adapting to changes in the inputs to the organization and the outputs demanded by the organization's environment. Because of the failure of JME's job rotation plan, employees have not been made to recognize that organizations are interdependent, not self-sufficient, and that they must respond to changes constantly occurring outside their boundaries. Furthermore, employees have not identified change in the organization of production as an ongoing process which occurs in response to feedback from one's environment rather than something that is planned to occur at discrete intervals. And finally, the attempted rotation has not promoted integration of thinking and doing rather than assigning managers responsibility for the former and workers responsibility for the latter.

> We have a lot of good workers, hard-working ones. However, Canadian workers' attention span is fairly narrow, tending to lack the holistic view. They don't seem to have a consciousness of relating their own work to all the others; they don't see the impact of their job on the rest of the system. They concentrate only on their own tasks. Even defects, they would rather let them go past, because they don't want to take responsibility for what someone has previously done. Workers in the same unit don't help each other, they don't respond to each others' mistakes, weaknesses, etc. Is that none of their business?

This observation was made by a Japanese senior manager. He recognizes that Canadian workers operate as though they are self-sufficient while Japanese workers recognize their interdependence. However, recognizing interdependence and the need to be responsive to others is, he seems to imply, culturally rather than structurally determined. The uniqueness of Canadian workers' behaviour is thus due to the individualist-oriented way of thinking, the individual worker being loyal to himself/herself first, and not to the work group in the way Japanese workers are. "Institutionalized behaviour differences" at the Simcoe Bay plant, therefore, were treated by JME's senior managers as a constraint which they were forced to accommodate by changing the structure – by not employing, for instance, job rotation in the way they would in Japan. They failed to recognize that by changing the structure to accommodate "institutionalized behaviour differences" they were depriving Canadian workers of the opportunity to learn that they can alter the way they coordinate their behaviour. Mutual adjustment, with its emphasis on developing responsiveness to those with whom one is interdependent, can replace rules which are designed to limit the need to coordinate with and respond to others. Canadians are not inherently incapable of coordinating their behaviour through mutual adjustment – they use this coordinating mechanism regularly within their families and when interacting with friends. However, factory workers are not used to coordinating their behaviour at work in this way, certainly not at the Simcoe Bay plant under Arcan. By limiting job rotation to accommodate "institutionalized behaviour differences," management limited the opportunity to recognize and comprehend the new expectations. As a result, workers continue to act on the basis of assumptions appropriate to the structure that they had under Arcan.

Rules of Seniority

The last issue which JME wished to negotiate with the union was the use of seniority as the sole determinant for internal movement within the operators' ranks. At Arcan straight seniority predominated in determining job assignments within both production and maintenance units as well as promotions and layoffs. Would seniority continue to determine one's access to positions in inter-departmental moves? Would workers move according to their own priorities or would such priorities become subordinate to those of the company? Could management come up with a system for assessing workers who have a greater number of skills and depth of knowledge, and for compensating them for their skills? These questions raised issues about the fit between the prevailing assumptions of the union's seniority system and those needed to create a flexible structure.

There is no question that workers felt and continue to feel strongly that seniority should determine one's eligibility to move from one job to another.

> They should go by seniority. A man has been here for so long he should get the better job. He's been here with this company; he's proven himself ... I can work, at my seniority and pick a job that fits my health and my ability to do that job ... I'd change it if I want to change, not because somebody else thinks I should.

According to some other employees, if seniority is not used,

> A supervisor gets the big say on what job you should do regardless of how hard you work or anything. If the supervisor takes a disliking to you or something, he can put you anywhere. You've got no say in the matter. You come in and do one job and the next night he can put you wherever he wants. So you spend all this time with this company and some student or

whatever comes in for the summer. They've got the good job and you've got the worst job. You like the security of knowing where you are going to be, where you stand.

The seniority principle has the merit of objectivity (Slichter et al., 1960), something which was emphasized by the union executives as well. They emphasized the workers' ability under the seniority system to control their own destiny by limiting the discretion of supervisors to reassign them to less worthy or less suitable work. However, for the management at JME the problems caused by this system of job assignments and promotion were described as more than "cultural shock," according to a Japanese manager. JME as an employer was now obliged to train the less qualified employee in order to enable him to take a job over a less senior employee who required no training. At the same time, a senior, more skilled employee could select only the easy work, leaving less well-trained, junior employees to handle the difficult assignments. Senior workers whose jobs were temporarily or permanently eliminated were allowed to "bump" junior employees from their jobs. Workers so displaced had the right to bump those junior to them and so on down the line (Doeringer and Piore:79). The manager in charge at JME presented the following case to explain the problem as he saw it:

> In the testing department we had eliminated 15 jobs with the introduction of new equipment. Those 15 people had to be provided other jobs in various departments. The outcome of this involved 60 people who had to be transferred among various sections! There are less than 400 people altogether.
> Of those, 60 were moving around at one point to comply with the job assignment rule based on seniority. In this system there is no element of selecting people at all. The chain of movement continues endlessly until when? Individuals' abilities or aptitudes as such are totally irrelevant in this way. People just move randomly. Only one's liking or disliking of a job counts? I think this system can seriously hinder production work.

A bump by one employee initiating a series of consecutive bumps down a progression is called chain bumping (Doeringer and Piore:55). It produces the greatest average number of reassignments per redundant employee, as in the case reported at JME. Doeringer and Piore pointed out that this introduces costs and frictions into the redundancy procedure since each move requires some retraining and reorientation to work. Also, in the eyes of Japanese managers, such large-scale reassignment of workers interferes with the ability of employees to acquire an in-depth knowledge of the production processes. People do not move through a sequence of job assignments custom-designed by their supervisor to provide increasing utilization of employees' skills. The concern here is that permitting people to shift on the basis of personal preference may result in underutilization of skills and may result in individual preference taking priority over organizational preferences. It may restrict management's ability to employ ability-first management, that is, "discovering the abilities of employees, developing these to the fullest, providing an environment, place and opportunity for them to be used and then rewarding them" (Cole, 1979: 133).

In a flexible-holistic approach, as Cole observed in the job structure of a Japanese auto plant he investigated, the gap between individual and organizational preferences is reduced; the probability that employee skills are underutilized as a result of seniority rights is also decreased. Operator and supervisor preferences usually converge since both seek to increase the worthiness of the operator's work. The operator seeks greater compensation associated with more worthy work while the supervisor seeks to develop the operator's skills to increase constantly his/her contribution to value added.

The problems of job classification, job rotation and seniority discussed in this chapter were found to be the most serious problem areas which JME has yet to resolve satisfactorily with its workers. Some respondents described these problems as "major failures" of the implementation process of Japanese management; they seem due to the overall failure on the part of JME to integrate technology with human resources. Shimada and MacDuffie (1987), in their recent review of Japanese automobile companies operating in the United States, stressed the linkage between the two systems in production. They argued that the Japanese uniqueness lies not in hardware technology alone, but in the interplay between technology and human resources that Japanese companies are attempting to introduce in their American plants. Their success or failure in North America thus seems largely dependent, the reasearchers imply, on how vigorously the attempt to implement the Japanese model is pursued by management and on the extent of institutionalization of the model attained. Figure 4.1 is the Japanese model of human resource management and industrial relations depicted by Shimada and MacDuffie.

Figure 4.1: JAPANESE MODEL OF HUMAN RESOURCE MANAGEMENT AND INDUSTRIAL RELATIONS

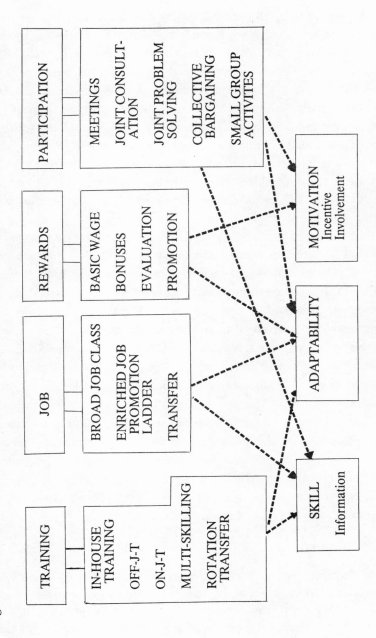

Source: Shimada, Haruo and John Paul MacDuffie, "Industrial Relations and 'Humanware': An Analysis of Japanese Investment in Automobile Manufacturing Industry in the United States," A Briefing Paper for the International Motor Vehicles Program.

56

Job restructuring, the reward system and promotion ladder, joint decision-making and training are identified as design factors in this model. Many aspects of the Japanese production system identified in this model which centre on human resource management were not introduced by JME at their Canadian plant; those introduced were either only partially done or not thoroughly and forcefully implemented. According to management the company intends to introduce some of these in the future, and has therefore only delayed introduction of those activities which seek to develop skill adaptability and motivation – human resource effectiveness (Figure 4.1). These factors may nonetheless have created conditions preventing the effective utilization of human resources and undermining the legitimacy of management in the eyes of employees.

Two other problems related to job structure remain thorny issues to be discussed at JME. The first has to do with the changing nature and content of jobs due to technological advances currently being made everywhere in the component manufacturing industry. The introduction of new technological methods and equipment by JME has created some jobs which are less complex as the work is made easier by the new machinery, and others which require greater skill and knowledge as the overseeing and maintenance of equipment becomes more complicated. The general trend in the industry at large is for maintenance or monitoring works to increase, and for routine-manual work to be replaced by machines. To increase productivity, JME's effort to automate the production system to the fullest extent will be continued, and in the process the number of manual jobs can only decrease. This process thus will have the effect of deskilling some workers while upgrading others. To accommodate these changes, it seems inevitable that the current job structure has to change sooner or later. Thus, it will continue to be in a state of flux for some years to come.

Work Customs

Another problem peculiar to the Simcoe Bay plant has to do with work customs. While job rotation was largely unknown to most of the employees at JME until the new management tried to introduce it, and "chain bumping" by seniority rule was a shocking phenomenon for the

Japanese to deal with, these issues can be regarded as an extension of work customs existing in manufacturing enterprises, as Doeringer and Piore (1971) elaborated – the problems caused by the differences in such customs at each workplace. People at different workplaces tend to generate a set of unwritten rules governing their actions and the relationship between themselves and outsiders. Rules "can govern any aspect of the work relationship from discipline to compensation" (Doeringer and Piore:23). Once rules are established custom begins to form around them through the process of application. If underlying conditions are stable, no conflict between efficiency and custom will emerge, and custom will not he recognized as a separate force, argued Doeringer and Piore.

One of the customs established at Simcoe Bay under the Arcan management was the practice of the so-called "half-on and half-off." This practice was accepted as "a reasonable way of doing jobs" by the union, management, and workers in general. In fact no conflict between efficiency and custom emerged until the new management took over the operation. This is how the practice was rationalized.

A very high percentage of the work at the plant is very repetitive and boring. Other jobs involve heavy lifting and are thus exhausting. Arcan's idea was to alleviate both these problems by having more people than were really needed so that a person could get away from the noise, the heat, and so on, and go for a break as he/she felt the need. Arcan's approach to discipline with reference to this custom was explained by one of the employees:

> As long as products were made, the management didn't care about anything else. They tell people what their job is and let them do it. Only if you are not doing it properly, would they come to you. If you can get your job done sooner by working harder or faster, you can take a break or you are free to do anything for the rest of your time. People liked the half-on and half-off thing. The cafeteria was full of people any time of the day.

The workers themselves decided how they were going to work and rest in compliance with the custom which was "unofficially accepted" by the management. There were various ways that the practice was exercised.

People's views on this work custom were somewhat mixed. It was a custom born as a "compromise" or "trade-off" which was worked out between the union and management in order to maintain harmony and stability on the shop floor. It was not sanctioned by the management; yet "they didn't know what to do about it." The half-on, half-off break system was a "tradition at Arcan" and "could not be changed." It was a "necessary and good thing," stated one of the ex-Arcan managers, because it helped both the quality and quantity. Workers produced a large number of products by this approach. Another ex-Arcan employee had a different view.

> It was a sign of very poor management at Arcan. It was accepted as the normal way. The workers liked it. They maybe worked a little harder when they were on the line. They could not keep up that pace all day, but there was no justification, not even in my view, for what they were doing. The whole thing was beginning to look ridiculous.

For the new JME management this customary procedure seemed inefficient and unacceptable from the perspective of discipline control. JME attempted to change this custom by importing two customs typical in Japanese industry: stricter time-keeping and line maintenance. Typically, it encountered real problems in trying to implement this change. Obviously, these problems stemmed in part from the real differences between Japanese and Western attitudes to the workplace. The Japanese approach to discipline in the workplace has been noted to be strict, and more forceful than would be accepted in many parts of Western industry (Dore, 1973; White and Trevor, 1983). The emphasis placed by Japanese companies on time keeping, for instance, was thought to be excessive by the British workers studied by White and Trevor, and the difference between Japanese-owned companies and other companies was reported to be larger in this particular respect.

JME followed other Japanese companies in taking a strict approach to discipline, in order to reduce carelessness and inefficiency. This was accompanied by the tighter staffing policy which is referred to at various points of discussion in this report. That Arcan was too easy-going and that no doubt some workers had taken advantage of this, was a widespread belief in the community, and JME's approach to discipline was in some ways a reaction to this. In the eyes of the JME managers, the Arcan practices enabled employees to leave the production line if there was a lull in the work. The plant manager explained the problem as JME perceived it:

> People spent 20 minutes in production and 20 minutes in the cafeteria. They actually worked for four hours instead of eight

hours. Once it becomes a way of life, you have a very difficult time reversing it or making significant change. You almost have to stop and start again, which is what we are doing. We have to get rid of the Arcan approach to the whole thing, both the management and employee attitude.

JME attempted to couple a stricter discipline with a greater emphasis on line clean-up. To keep one's place at work tidy is a norm accepted by practically everyone in any work organization in Japan. It is a common practice for a worker in a factory to clean up the line before he/she leaves it. This work custom was "imported" to the Simcoe Bay plant by the Japanese staff, who instructed workers to spare some time during the overlapping between shifts cleaning and tidying the area. The management noted that this practice would reduce the size of caretaking staff substantially, and hoped that negative reaction from their workers would be of short duration.

Eliminating the half-on, half-off custom has been resented by some of the work force, because they feel they are being "pushed around." The new "janitorial services" which have been assigned are perceived as "extra work without pay" which should not be a part of their job. "A job is a job, not two or three jobs to do." As JME has discovered, widely held customs are not easily changed even by a new employer; such changes can lead to worker dissatisfaction and resentment.

This chapter has revealed the conflict and resulting compromise between the Japanese and Canadian systems involving a variety of job-related issues. Conflict and compromise are inherent in processes of change and accomodation in any organization. A considerable amount of learning and relearning and of continuous trail-and-error seems to be required on the part of both management and workers. The future shape of the job structure at the Simcoe Bay plant thus appears to be dependent on further union-management negotiations. What shape it finally takes still remains to be seen.

Chapter Five
The Changing Role of the Supervisor

The production department of the Simcoe Bay plant under Arcan management had two levels of supervision: superintendents and foremen. JME has created only one category of supervision, people whom they call supervisors for the functions of direct supervision in production. In thinning the bureaucratic structure the company has not only eliminated Arcan's middle supervisory position of superintendents, but also substantially reduced the number of technical support staff (Chapter Three). Supervisors are now expected to perform the traditional role of foremen in addition to other management functions.

All the supervisors whose roles were examined by means of interview and questionnaire in this study were part of the system of control over production. There were sixteen such supervisors (of whom fifteen were male and one female) at the time of the data collection. All of them were ex-Arcan employees, the majority having been in supervisory positions previously and some in technical-support positions. Two of them were promoted by JME to be supervisors after some work experience as shop-floor operators. Each one of them was interviewed by the researcher in the early stages of this study.

The literature on the subject has demonstrated that technology and the way that work is organized determine the substance of supervision. Goldthorpe (1959) in his early study on the mining industry in Great Britain noted the changing functions of supervisors in the industry by comparing the pre-mechanization or 'hand-got' system in the nineteenth and early twentieth centuries, the partially mechanized or 'conventional' production, and the fully mechanized system of coal mining. Each technological stage had its own form of supervision.

With the coming of the assembly line, the responsibilities of supervisors or foremen became generally reduced (Walker and Guest, 1952). The conveyor imposes the pace of work, directs the sequence of materials and tools to be used and determines the output, without much intervention from the supervisor. At the same time, new responsibilities for supervisors arise. Because of increased absenteeism and labour turnover they have constantly to train new workers, obtain replacements, provide tools and watch closely the supply of materials. They also have to ensure the proper quality of products. The major task of the supervisor in the area of people supervision has thus been transformed from directing and checking on subordinates to helping them and to being their trouble-shooter.

Woodward (1965), in her pioneering work on technology and management, provided the characteristics of mass production by noting a wide span of control; on the average there were fifty people under one supervisor in the data she collected in Great Britain. The lowest span of control was seen to be in the process operation, reflecting the need for supervisor surveillance of high-speed production processes to ensure that product runs were error-free.

As production becomes more computer-controlled, a supervisor spends less time monitoring production processes. Increased attention is devoted to integrating production processes more effectively and redesigning processes so that existing resources are more fully utilized. Improving coordination and allocating resources more efficiently become increasingly important, and attention is focused on using the information generated by information systems to improve these allocative and coordinating decisions. Increasingly, supervisors manage resources and processes rather than people. Consequently, supervisors in new technologies, a pilot study recently conducted in the United States suggests, tend more to identify themselves with management than they used to, for they are a greater part of managerial decision-making and a more integral part of the decision-making process (Grimm and Dunn, 1986).

In an earlier chapter we reported that the supervisor-worker ratio was somewhat higher at JME than at Arcan. As the supervisors have become increasingly responsible for production, more so under the JME management than Arcan, they supervise machines more, and people less. Their main concerns are controlling quality and dealing with the operating contingencies that influence the performance of the production process.

With a broader base and fewer staff specialists at JME the function of supervisors and the scope of their authority have been widened. They must impose more work pressure and discipline on their workers than did their Arcan counterparts. While Arcan had both a technician and a foreman in each work section on each shift, at JME supervisors must supervise people and be knowledgeable about every facet of the operation. At the time our interviews with supervisors were being conducted, machinery was frequently being adapted to deal with the new lines of production introduced by JME; breakdowns often occurred, and the supervisors spent a large part of their time making minor alterations to machinery. They were also somewhat pressured by the demands of production, devoting much of their energy to meeting schedules and overcoming blockages which threatened the continuity of production. Veteran supervisors described the changes they were experiencing in their roles:

> The Japanese expect you to work 100% or 120% all the time. It's not enough for you to come in, work 8 hours and go home. A supervisor with JME has to be involved in supervision of people and also have the knowledge of the engineering process. You are supposed to do both. So the role of the supervisor has been changed; the territory of the job is greater. We are doing two jobs. While Arcan had two people or in some cases four people, we now have one. It's hard to get used to, but it's a challenge more than anything else to me.

> The job is demanding. You have the people responsibility and then the machine responsibility. Responsibility for the people comes first, but there is lots of work to be done on the machines. I'm always too busy. Right now I look after the area on the off-shift. I'm the only one. There are only four supervisors in the whole plant on the off-shift. That's a lot of people to look after.

With Arcan you did not concentrate on the technical part. You always had a technician in the department. In JME a supervisor is also a technician. Sometimes I feel the JME way is better. It's more interesting. But it can become difficult to handle when you have two departments to look after on night shifts.

The quotations cited above indicate that JME's supervisors are conscious of the changes in the supervisory role associated with increased mechanization, but not of those associated with the transition from mechanically- to electronically-controlled systems. They have not yet adjusted to the supervisory roles which develop when computer-controlled information systems are used. Many of the supervisors still prefer the hierarchical, top-down system characteristic of Arcan.

An Arcan supervisor worked for a superintendent who was on shift all the time. A supervisor reported to him whenever he had any problem in coordinating the plan. Now you are entirely on your own. We report to the production manager, but he is not here at night.

Reporting back to their superiors is one of the things supervisors at JME do every day as they did at Arcan. At JME an estimated two hours a day of the supervisor's time is spent on reports and entering data into the computer system. More time is also spent in meetings with managers. Supervisors are also under pressure to reduce the amount of time they spend in error detection and control – in direct monitoring of employees.

The job is harder. We spend less time supervising people now than we did. We spend two hours a day now doing paper work, entering numbers into a computer, which is really a clerical job in an office. I am not doing my job well enough as a supervisor. If something goes wrong in the process, it may not be picked up. I feel that you should be in your work area all the time or at least 90% of your time. I think you should be spending a lot of time monitoring the process, as we don't have QC personnel any more.

Duties assigned to supervisors at the Simcoe Bay plant seem heavy, even "heavier than those to which foremen are assigned in our plant in Japan," the production manager admitted. A supervisor's job at JME is close to the one of sub-foreman or sub-section head in Japan, a person who directs day-to-day operations on the shop floor the large majority of his time, and to whom workers turn for help when a problem arises. Above a sub-foreman in large Japanese factories is usually a foreman who spends most of his time attending to paper work in his office with occasional tours of the shop floor to make sure everything is running smoothly. Moreover, in Japan the actual work of supervision, which in a Western company would have been done by a single set of foremen, is shared by employees in a number of ranks. Clark (1979: 191) reported that there were machine leaders, team leaders and the supervisor (sub-section head) who were each responsible for a part of the shop floor in the factory he investigated. The various leaders were appointed informally on the understanding that they would assist the supervisor whenever the need arose. This system would be difficult to implement in a Canadian plant, where informal and mutual assistance is not established as a custom and where such a job definition cannot be initiated under the current labor contract with the union. At JME, because the company has not developed the team leader system, workers have not assumed responsibility for gathering and filtering suggestions or for improving safety and equipment maintenance. Workers have taken on some of the training functions which were performed by supervisors, but they have not taken on the tasks associated with assisting co-workers, not only because of inadequate team experience, but also because they believe that vertical decentralization has not occurred.

The increased duties and responsibilities that the supervisors are expected to carry are no doubt "hard and heavy for any one to take," as one of them told the researcher, and are also for many of them alien to their experience. The impression we received when talking with supervisors was that they were experiencing a great deal of anxiety and disturbance. Many felt that they were overloaded with organizational requirements, and that they were unable to communicate their problems and difficulties to their superiors. On the whole they were working hard, but always under pressure. The sense of loss and helplessness which they expressed is explained partly because, unlike the old days, nothing is stable and certain in the current operation. The jobs change, and "what is right today may be wrong tomorrow." Management often fails to explain the reasons for its action or take steps to reassure the supervisor.

One supervisor described his experience as "surviving from day to day," and another declared that "any job at this plant other than the supervisor's" was desirable to him and he was ready to change places. A few saw the improvement in the operation as the new lines and equipment were getting well established, and found their supervisory role with JME interesting. These people could afford to appreciate greater responsibility and a wider range of job functions. "No two days are alike. There is always something different." "I like the variety of my job, different problems all the time, a heck of a lot of pressure though." Asked whether they found the time they had spent at work with Arcan more or less interesting than their present work, about half of them (seven out of sixteen) reported that they found their time at work with JME more interesting than that it had been with Arcan. For five of them the time was more interesting with Arcan. The remaining four saw no difference; "supervisors are supervisors wherever you are."

The supervisors at JME often find themselves caught 'in the middle' between two different organizational structures (Gardner and Whyte, 1945). On the one hand, they maintain daily contact with their subordinates, whom they supervise. Subordinates are Canadian and expect supervision to be exercised along usual lines and standards. On the other hand, they are exposed to the pressures of their superiors from whom they receive instructions and orders, and who happen to be Japanese. The conflicting requiements which they experience were discussed extensively by the supervisors in the course of their interview.

> I think it is still the culture that rules here – the Japanese way. Over there [in Japan] I think employees start working together from the beginning; they help each other automatically. In Canada you can't bring in a man and say 'you are going to do this; you are going to help that person.' Right away there is resentment. That is not because they don't want to work, but because of the culture that they were brought up in and because of unions in this country.

> Over there [in Japan] workers on the line would do repairs to equipment. Our people are not trained to do that. Union says that they don't have to. But Japanese expect it. Their expectations are wrong. They have to change them. I don't ask people to do many things requested by management, because it's not safe. People do not have enough knowledge to

be assured about the safety. They are not qualified to do the job.

While Arcan really didn't want operators tinkering with machines, JME likes employees to get involved in small maintenance problems. They want them to get involved in getting proper techniques. The union wouldn't let the people learn their work – protectionism of other jobs. If the workers see what causes the problem, it would be much easier for them to react to it, and solve it.

JME expects more from employees. The employees are not used to working on their own. They think they are still working under supervision; 'You tell me what to do. You watch me in case I don't do right.' They have to be told what to do and be looked after. We have to baby sit. Now they have to be on their own, i.e., in quality control as the new management insists. Most of the employees worked with Arcan too long. They trusted Arcan, their way of doing things.

A worker in a Japanese plant is not merely an operator of machines. A worker controls a good portion of the machinery and equipment; he sets it up, runs it, and maintains it. A worker is expected and trained to be a skilled worker for any type of job employing any process. In Japan workers are multi-skilled or multi-functioned (Monden, 1983), and according to the supervisors Japanese managers at the Simcoe Bay plant do expect workers to be the same. This expectation is wrong and dangerous since it may lead a belief that they can build increasing responsibility into their Canadian workers' jobs without adequate provisions, i.e., without proper education and training.

Under the former employer, Arcan, the workers on the shop floor were single - functioned workers. They worked as specialists at a certain type of job. "Tinkering with machines" was not expected or desired. "You just didn't see a worker running and fixing machines." Jobs were organized with a standard performance output established for each job. The relationship between the individual and the job was one to one, the goal being to ensure accountability. Helping co-workers complete their task, under such arrangements, could involve a violation of rules of the union, if not of the company. In Japanese firms, however, the ideology and cultural values stress cooperative group activity. Thus, it was a great surprise to a Japanese manager to find that workers in the same group did not help each other. A worker does not respond even to "a fellow worker standing next to him who is in trouble." The concept of a team or workgroup in Canada does not connote togetherness or mutual help, which, in Japanese minds, is a natural part of behaviour expected in any work organization. As one of the supervisors cited above observed, these conceptual differences result from institutionalized patterns of behaviour appropriate to each of the societies. Members of organizations in Japan are expected to work together from the beginning till retirement in compliance with the norm of lifetime employment.

The supervisors' comment, on the disparity between reality and the Japanese concept of worker role also suggest that they themselves lack many of the skills needed to function effectively under the new management. They have not assumed responsibility for developing team skills through task assignment and reassignment. They could be more creative in assigning broader tasks to individual workers or in moving them among various tasks depending on their approach to skill development and job design. Some of them are still inclined to write off the notion that workers can and do work effectively on their own. The literature in the field has provided ample evidence that workers like to make suggestions for change and even to assume some staff functions. Like many workers elsewhere, the most consistent complaint the workers at JME expressed was the failure of supervisors to listen to suggestions. The supervisors do not see that they could collaborate with their subordinates to improve coordination and to use resources more effectively.

Neither the supervisors nor workers seem to have adequately understood the consequences of technological change for their roles. There is an assumption on the part of the supervisor that workers resist changes, and when they encounter the slightest resistence they tend to abandon redefinition of the approach rather than explaining why and how roles are changing. Because technological change is still underway, in fact will be a constant process at JME for some time to come, supervisors and workers alike must begin working more closely together to adapt their jobs and responsibilities to these changes.

JME supervisors also pointed to a second aspect of Japanese expectations that are in conflict with those of Canadian workers. These concern the differences in the concept of or attitudes toward work. During the course of the interviews practically every one of the supervisors made reference at one point or another to the significance of the value system, pointing out that what work means to Japanese workers can be quite different from what it means to Canadaian workers. The difference is understood conceptually, but not in reality by Japanese managers.

> Here there is always a person who says; 'I'm here only for money.' Everybody is not equally conscientious. In Japan people are working for their company. The company is their life. The company looks after them. In Canada you haven't got that.

> With a lesser number of workers, they are so busy. They don't have time to spend with somebody else. This is the way they run it over there [in Japan]. Being a different class of people, that doesn't work here. They think nothing of working 12 or 16 hours a day whereas we more or less put in 8 hours a day. That's the way we live. Japanese can't change it.

> JME is very different. The principles they use are not the principles I had used before or that I learned at school. The assumed dedication of Japanese workers cannot be assumed in Canada. Employees in Canada must be motivated so that they want to work. Otherwise they won't. In Japan, I believe, they'll work.

> There is no concern about employee morale or how people feel. Japanese think that workers are all motivated. It is taken for granted. It cannot be taken for granted. I'll go to Mr. S [the Japanese manager] to talk about a technical problem, but I don't even consider talking to him about people problems. How could I tell him 'I have a motivation problem with my people?'

> Canadian workers' attitudes would be a problem for JME. JME runs based on their thinking how the operation runs in Japan. They try to instill the same thing here. However, workers' attitudes are already instilled from the previous employer. That makes my job difficult to do.

The views of Japanese workers cited above are typical of those held by the Canadian supervisors in our study. Other frequently made remarks were that for Japanese "work is their whole life, more important than anything else"; Japanese workers think "nothing of working 12 or 16 hours day, being born to be work-oriented." Overall Japanese workers were perceived to be more highly motivated to work than were their Canadian counterparts. The statements almost always had an implication that workers in other countries are otherwise. People in Canada go to work because they have to earn a living, not because they love to work. There are always enough people who say 'I am here only for money.' The eight-hour workday is a norm of work in the "recreational life-oriented" community of Simcoe Bay, unlike, for instance, the neighboring metropolitan area, according to a few interviewees. The family and recreational life are important for the people in the area and "come before work" to the workers. If this is true, then it is clear that employees in Canada must be motivated to a far greater extent than employees in Japan, a principle of supervision which has been downgraded or treated lightly by the Japanese management up to now.

Are views put forth by these supervisors merely stereotypes? How realistic is their portrayal of employee attitudes? The questionnaire did not include questions specifically designed to measure worker attitudes and committment to work, and it is impossible to present an exact corroboration from the questionnaire for the views expressed by supervisors and other responding workers. However, enough general questions designed to gain a broad understanding of worker attitude were included to give us some idea of how workers would assess the remarks of their supervisors.

Asked whether they felt that their work was worthwhile, a valuable part of their life, or it was just something they do to earn a living, more than half (fifty-two per cent) of the responding workers indicated that they work only to earn a living; for thirty-seven per cent of the respondents their work is worthwhile, while the remaining ten per cent were not sure. About twenty-eight per cent of respondents find themselves 'often' thinking, when they start off for work, 'I don't want to go in today.' Another thirty-eight per cent find this to be the case 'sometimes,' twenty-five per cent rarely, and another ten per cent never. We have little comparable data from other samples of workers in similar industries which would help us to assess how typical these responses are relative to workers in other parts of the country.

One of the conclusions reached by Cole (1979:237), in his reconceptualizing the empirical findings on the Japanese work ethic, was that Japanese workers tend to show a greater need to find fulfillment in work relative to employees in other nations. There is ample evidence that Japanese workers show unusually high levels of identification with the company. Nonetheless, Cole argues, this higher identification does not mean that they are fully committed to the specific work tasks that they are performing. Thus, American workers studied by Cole (1979:233) showed a higher level of commitment to their work than their Japanese counterparts. Asked whether or not they would go into the same kind of work they were doing now, if they could do it all over again, fifty-four per cent of Cole's Detroit respondents would choose the same work if they had it to do over again, compared to thirty-three per cent of the Yokohama employees. These percentage figures are considerably higher than those of the JME employees in Simcoe Bay in Canada because only one out of five (nineteen per cent) of them indicated that they would choose the same kind of work.

The points made by the supervisors are, first, that there exists fundamental differences between Japanese and Canadian workers in their attitudes toward work. In sum, as Dore (1982) described, Japanese workers are more inclined to be "membership motivated." Thus, workers are more likely to offer their ideas and extra efforts to promote the company's success because of their sense of belonging to the firm. In the West workers are more inclined to be "market motivated" and thus to say that "I do what I am paid to, no less but no more." As this motivational difference is not something which can be spontaneously wiped out with a change of management, the supervisors insisted, secondly, that Japanese management should realize that "they are not dealing with a same type or class of people," and should act accordingly. The Japanese assume that worker commitment and cooperation automatically exist at any workplace, including their Canadian plant. They don't question worker motivation; it is taken for granted, when in reality it cannot be.

In Japanese corporations membership motivation is derived from institutional arrangements: the permanent employment system, the emphasis on in-company training, career orientation of workers, payment by age and length of service, and enterprise-based unions. With no such institutional arrangements in their Canadian environment, how can management act and run the factory based on the assumption of membership motivation? This issue is complicated further by the role that unions play in Western corporations in general, and at JME in particular. The Japanese appear to use great caution and sensitivity in dealing with union-related issues, but they are still largely in the stage of familiarizing themselves with the institutional arrangements made under unionization in this country. The very notion that management and workers act with a premise of opposed interests is basically foreign to the Japanese. Thus, while the message that "the union at this plant was, and has always been strong and difficult to deal with," is there; in the view of some Canadian supervisors the Japanese managers do not always understand its implications.

The questions raised by the issue of worker motivation are thus very real. Are there indeed fundamental cultural differences in attitudes toward work that JME management must address? Or could workers change their attitudes toward work if the consequences of technological changes for their roles are adequately understood? The argument that employees must continuously be motivated in order to work assumes the existence of high vertical and horizontal specialization. It assumes that the supervisor must compensate for the way work is organized to alleviate consequences of deskilling. And in fact this is the assumption that supervisors at JME seem to be labouring under. They have not understood, possibly because management has not helped them to understand, that as the organization of work increases in both breadth and depth when workers become involved in multi-functional capabilities, the supervisor does not have to compensate as much for the organization of work. Rather, supervision can change its focus to more effective utilization of human resources – skill development, job redesigning, and so on. Supervision must also provide opportunities for those employees who enjoy working together in a team to work in concert. Unfortunately, the understanding of this fact seems to have escaped the supervisors at the Simcoe Bay plant.

Role conflict and role ambiguity lead to uncertainty about what one is expected to do in one's job (Wray, 1949) and it is exactly this kind of uncertainty which seems to be affecting the supervisors at JME. Studies show that the incidence of ulcers among foremen tends to be disproportionately high, which is a symptom of the stress built into the foreman's job (Warr and Wall, 1975). The Simcoe Bay workers are aware of the fact that their supervisors are under constant pressure at the time of the study; a rumour was being circulated within the plant that a few of their bosses had had minor heart attacks due to the heavy pressures. The large majority of the supervisors in the study indicated that they found their work worthwhile, yet at the same time stressful. Every one of the supervisors without exception asserted that their job has become more stressful under JME due to their increased responsibility coupled with the conflicting requirements already built into their role. To the question "If a problem comes up at work which is not settled when you go home, how often do you find yourself thinking about it after work?" ten out of sixteen supervisors replied that they found themselves thinking 'often' about the unsettled problems even after work.

The problems that the supervisors are experiencing in fulfilling the increased responsibilities and in coping with role conflict and ambiguity derive in large part from the differences in the way the work is organized under the two management systems. JME's management orientation is close to what Burns and Stalker (1961) termed the organic system. It assumes that conditions surrounding the plant operation are in constant change, and that production processes are changing rather than fixed. Because change constantly gives rise to fresh problems and unforeseen requirements for action, management assumes that rules must be flexible. Action plans and rules cannot simply be written down and distributed automatically. Given this scenario, the supervisor's role in handling these changes must be to implement the changes at the task level and ensure that new machinery and tools operate correctly, that workers understand the new process and that quality standards are maintained under the new technology.

This organic approach seems harder for some supervisors to get used to than others.

> We don't seem to have structure. I'm not sure what organizational system we have here. We even don't understand what the set-up is. For production management Arcan used to have a production manager on the floor. From there he used to give his directives to a superintendent, and a superintendent turned them over to a foreman. There was an obvious chain of command.

> Arcan's structure from top management down was precise. With Arcan you knew exactly what the structure was, and what you were expected to do within that structure. Everything was clearly defined. With JME there is no structure, no system, no nothing. I liked the Arcan structure. Now you don't know what the function of managers or supervisors is. Here

> supervisors are floating. You don't know whether you do have
> the responsibility or not. You are not sure what you are
> supposed to do. Even if you ask, you don't get a clear answer.

> I don't feel any sense of direction and that really makes me
> unhappy. Even if some sort of direction is given to us, the
> whole concept will be changed the next week. I don't have a
> lot of confidence in the management right now. With Arcan I
> was more secure. I could see where we were going. I need to
> get some directions, something more concrete from the people
> above me. We weren't given information even on weekly
> requirements. There was no way of knowing them.

Since the new management stresses flexibility rather than
standardization, less horizontal and vertical specialization is employed. This
approach has increased the discretion not only of first-line supervisors, but
also of workers. Not all supervisors perceive this increased discretion as
desirable. Obviously, quite a few still cling to "the Arcan ways" and refuse to
accept the new. A young engineer hired by JME typifies the resistance to the
change among his colleagues and supervisors alike:

> Japanese started introducing new things one by one. The
> Canadian staff are not willing to accept them. You often hear
> a Canadian manager saying he'll run things in the way he likes,
> because he doesn't understand what's going on anyway. Some
> engineers or process specialists won't touch some of the new
> equipment because they are afraid. They say that it should not
> have come here in the first place. If a person resists new
> equipment even before he sees it, you can't change that
> person's mind.

This resistance may range from passive resistance in which there is a general
indifference to the new ideas so that nothing is ever done about them, to
active denial of the value of the new (Burns and Stalker). A few of the JME
supervisors were rather blunt about their resistance to change. In some cases
these individuals tried to defend the Arcan technology against the new
technology being introduced by JME. They showed a strong distrust of
management, and felt that they were subject to arbitrary demands from
above and that they were given no consideration.

It is clear, therefore, that the organic form of management that JME
has been attempting to establish in its Simcoe Bay plant has caused as much
anxiety for the local employees as for the Japanese. Confusion has arisen
from a disparity in expectations and assumptions which have neither been

communicated nor discussed. Japanese expatriates expressed their disappointment with local staff, managers and supervisors:

> They [Canadian managers and supervisors] are not responding to the changes fast enough and flexibly enough in our view. They do only assigned tasks just like the operators. They do not go beyond the scope of their responsibility and territory. They must have their responsibilities clearly defined and work only with those definitions.

And yet the literature posits that a certain amount of confusion and anxiety is inevitable in the transition to an organic form of organization. Managers and supervisors may indeed "yearn for more definition and structure" as Burns and Stalker (1961: 122-123) elaborated:

> The organic form, by departing from the familiar clarity and fixety of the hierarchic structure, is often experienced by the individual manager as an uneasy, embarrassed, or chronically anxious quest for knowledge about what he should be doing, or what is expected of him, and similar apprehensiveness about what others are doing ... this kind of response is necessary if the organic form of organization is to work effectively.

JME's management should understand the inevitability of the confusion and work at increasing their communications with supervisors to overcome this problem. Supervisors should be made aware of ways that they can make their own jobs easier by communicating in turn with the workers. The inevitable changes in workers' jobs due to changing technology do not necessarily have to be construed as a hardship by workers, as they too often are at the moment.

Given this confusion, and the fact that they are constantly overwhelmed by "all sorts of problems in production," how are supervisors behaving in the eyes of other employees in the plant? How are they being evaluated by their subordinates? Workers were asked to rate their supervisors in terms of eleven characteristics.[1] A cluster analysis of these indicates the existence of two interpretable clusters based on nine of the questions: personal consideration and work facilitation. Two characteristics of the supervisory behaviour were not part of the two clusters identified in the cluster analysis. The questions included in each cluster and the distribution of the responses are given in Table 5.1.

Table 5.1: Worker Evaluation of Supervisory Behaviour – JME (N = 241)

Behaviour	Percentages		
	Very likely	Somewhat likely	Unlikely
My supervisor is: Personal Consideration			
to help subordinates with personal problems	35.0%	41.2%	23.9%
to be fair with subordinates	44.4	39.9	15.6
to treat each subordinate as an important individual	41.7	39.0	19.3
to be concerned about me as a person	42.0	37.7	20.4
Work Facilitation			
to encourage participation in important decisions	28.5	48.3	23.3
to defend subordinates to "higher ups"	31.5	48.4	20.2
to evaluate my performance accurately	53.2	33.7	13.2
to be trustworthy	56.1	30.5	13.4
to behave competently	56.1	33.6	10.3
Other[*]			
to demand that people give their best effort	63.5	28.7	7.8
to leave it up to me to decide how to go about my job	44.3	40.8	14.9

[*] These two aspects of supervisory behaviour were not part of any of the two clusters identified in the cluster analysis.

It is safe to state that overall the workers at JME seemed rather critical of the behaviour of their supervisors. Figures in the table indicate that the JME supervisors were perceived by their subordinates as fairly demanding bosses; sixty-four per cent of the reporting workers said that it was very likely that their supervisor demanded their best effort of them. These bosses were at the same time less likely to encourage participation in important decisions and to defend them to "higher ups"; only about thirty per cent of the employees said that their supervisors would do so.

In an earlier American study, Quinn and Shepard (1974) interviewed 1,496 members of the U.S. labour force using a national probability sample of dwellings. A set of fifteen questions in the survey dealt specifically with worker evaluation of supervisors. A few of the characteristics used in the American study are close enough to the ones used in the present study for comparison. The comparative percentage figures from the two studies with the respective questions are presented in Table 5.2 (the two sample groups are not exactly identical, as the American study included some salaried workers with identifiable supervisors).

In terms of competence, JME supervisors were relatively favourably evaluated by their subordinates; fifty-six per cent of them reported that it was very likely that their supervisor behaved competently; whereas the seventy-two per cent, or fifteen per cent more, of the respondents surveyed by Quinn and Shepard said that it was very true that their supervisor knew his/her own job well. It has been noted in the field (Gust, 1971) that supervisors are generally less favorably evaluated; a statement commonly heard is that the best form of supervision from the worker's point of view is one where the foreman is never seen on the shop floor (Goldthorpe, et al., 1968:64-65). It has become more or less normal for employees not to raise their expectations about their supervisor. Our findings may simply reflect the low levels of expectation that JME workers have come to accept as normal.

Among the four characteristics of supervisory behaviour we have compared, JME employees gave an unusually low rating to decision-making. Less than thirty per cent of the workers reported that their supervisors encouraged participation in decision-making (whereas at least forty-one per cent of the American respondents reported that their supervisor encouraged

Table 5.2: Comparison of Supervisory Behaviour

Behaviour	Very likely	Somewhat likely	Unlikely
JME			
My supervisor is:			
to behave competently	56.15%	33.65%	10.35%
to demand that people give their best effort	63.5	28.7	7.8
to leave it up to me to decide how to go about my job	44.3	40.8	14.9
to encourage participation in important decisions	28.5	48.3	23.3

The American National Sample Survey[*]			
Supervisor:	Very true	Somewhat true	Not true
Knows his/her own job well	71.6%	19.1%	9.3%
Encourages those he/she supervises to give their best effort	67.3	35.3	7.4
Lets those he/she supervises alone unless they want help	59.9	28.7	11.3
Encourages those he/she supervises to exchange opinions and ideas	42.1	30.8	27.1

[*]Source: Quinn, Robert P. and Linda J. Shepard, *The 1972-73 Quality of Employment Survey*, Ann Arbor, Michigan. University of Michigan, Survey Research Center, 1974. p. 200-201.

them to exchange opinions and ideas). This low evaluation by JME workers may indicate that many of their supervisors have not adopted the participative style of supervision expected by the new management. Makabe (1983) in her study conducted in Toronto found that local employees employed by Japanese firms could not function effectively within the "Japanese style of participatory decision making" due to their own assumptions about managerial behaviour. Nightingale (1982) also noted that many of the supervisors in his study were still following the principles of the 'command-and-obey' type of supervision of an earlier era, finding it difficult to adopt the participative style demanded in the democratic organizations.

While JME supervisors were evaluated as being relatively competent by their subordinates, the Japanese management noted the variations in work performance and attitudes toward work in general of their supervisors. There are "a few excellent people, and a few who are just not making it." The disparity between the two extreme groups is seen as substantial and causes Japanese managers some difficulty in working effectively with their Canadian supervisors.   This disparity in supervisor performance is something unfamiliar to them, since the Japanese are used to working with homogeneous groups of employees, whichever the group may be. The weakness in supervisory-managerial skills amongst some supervisors has been noted as a "serious problem." The problem is most clearly revealed when new duties are added to the work of the supervisors by JME, a concrete example being holding daily shift meetings.

Shift meetings are held at the end of one production shift and at the start of another shift by having half-an-hour overlapping between the two shifts. That means employees spend an extra half-hour in addition to the regular eight hours on each shift. Meetings are intended to be used to discuss difficult problems, features of the shift's work that day, changes of rules, or special steps required that have to be planned in advance. The major activities of other sections and departments can also be communicated through the meetings. According to the plant manager, shift meetings permit communication and consultation between the supervisors and workers freed from the constraints of work. They permit mutual adjustment and encourage the flexibility needed in production because procedures are not fully standardized.

While the meetings were reported to have been successful in producing substantial improvements in productivity and yields within some parts of the organization, their purpose has not been widely understood nor accepted. "We don't see how this overlapping benefits anyone" is a comment heard quite often from both workers on the floor and supervisors. As a consequence, in some areas no meetings are held at all; either supervisors decide not to have them, or the members of the unit see "no reasons to gather in a meeting, so we don't have a meeting." Twenty-four per cent of the respondents said that overlapping time was not spent for meetings in their department. Of those employees who reported that meetings were held regularly, nine per cent reported that meetings introduced by JME were very useful, forty per cent that they were somewhat useful, and fifteen per cent that they were not useful at all. In admitting the difficulty in handling the daily meeting, some supervisors gave the following reasons for this difficulty:

> Everyday at the beginning of the shift I tell my people as to what products are coming down, anything special to look for, rule changes, etc. A meeting helps, but some people have figured out that it's a waste of time. As a supervisor I have to convince my people that it can be useful. It's not easy.

> I've a meeting, not all the time. Usually I go around to individuals and talk with them. I'm closer to people because I work with them. In a group setting, they usually don't say that much.

> I think a meeting has been a failure. There is never enough time for me to do all that I am supposed to do during the overlapping. I circulate among operators during the shift, asking their personal problems, etc., if they have any. I get better results by doing so. Trying to cram it in a 10-15 minute meeting, you don't get the answers back. I think workers do respond to the personal approach much better than the formal approach.

> Overlapping means an extra half an hour for people. It is the time when they are supposed to do cleaning the area [sic], tidying, etc. In my work area we have meetings once in a while. We just don't seem to look into it. I can see the theory behind the meeting. I agree with it. Whether it will ever get into practice is another question. The theory is fine, provided

everyone is motivated to do right up the job [sic] and want to improve their lot and the lot of the company.

I don't have meetings every day. I don't sit down with them for a half-an-hour meeting. If I find a problem, I decide to have a meeting with all shifts that I look after, so that they all get the same message. It does help. The objectives are good, but with Canadian workers, it is not well accepted. They sit there and listen. Whether it's getting there or not, you cannot tell. You don't get a lot of contributions from them.

I find the meeting hard. You cannot have a meeting with people every single day. You have to set up jobs for people to kill their 20 to 30 minutes. You can ask them or tell them to do something. Otherwise they don't do anything. They are not getting paid for the extra time. There are certain things you can talk about, but I don't see why half an hour every day. I think it's a waste of time.

In attempting to explain why such meetings have been considerably less fruitful than expected, the Japanese managers have assumed that supervisors lack the managerial skills needed to effectively preside over such meetings. Both supervisors and workers seem unable to talk things out freely or feel uncomfortable doing so. Managers in other Japanese-managed firms interviewed by Makabe also commented that the level of discussion at the departmental meetings involving both managerial and non-managerial staff was not high to their great disappointment: "Canadian workers seem somewhat uncomfortable about participating in those meetings, and remain uninterested in them" (Makabe, 1983:28).

The view shared by Japanese managers is that the problem is more with the supervisors than the workers at JME: "They don't know what to discuss and how to lead the discussion. The overlapping time can be beneficial and the meeting can become effective when the supervisors are trained in inter-personal and communicative skills."

No doubt the supervisors' lack of skills is a problem, but more so is the inability of both supervisors and workers to identify such meetings as an alternative coordinating mechanism – one which mobilizes the expertise of the team to redesign work. Until workers recognize that continual adaptation of production processes is required, and that it is their responsibility to propose changes in the division and design of work, this coordinating mechanism will function poorly and the worker's role will continue to be poorly understood. Under such circumstances improvements in productivity and yeild will be delayed.

Management has not developed a team leadership system yet. Because the supervisors still lack many of the skills needed to function effectively as internal communication specialists, small group processes have not been implemented. Since supervisors are still acting as linking pins rather than as internal communication specialists, more emphasis is placed on one-way downward communication, not on two-way communication. The supervisors' comments clearly indicate the situation, and provide the reasons why they deal with their people individually rather than in groups and why shift meetings are not working. The fact that decision-making behaviour of supervisors is not favourably evaluated by the workers at JME is consistent with this reality.

For the Japanese, communication and information-sharing are the most important facets of management, and the shift meetings at their Canadian plant are thus too important as a means of maintaining communication channels among various segments of the organization to bargain away. The limited success of meetings so far has been a great disappointment to the JME's management; nonetheless, they seem to be determined to make this system work and have it established as a normal working practice within the plant. It is to be hoped that they can find the means to communicate the importance of these meetings to both supervisors and workers.

In this chapter the discussion has been focussed on the impact of technology on roles and duties performed by a supervisor, the central figure in supervision of production work. The notion that has emerged is that technology changes the role of the supervisor, and that as technology changes, the role must change too. The supervisors at the Simcoe Bay plant have been going through the transition period with a fair amount of strain and pain because they do not understand the consequences of technological change on roles which they are still getting used to. It may take some time for the supervisors to adjust to these changes, but they must adjust sooner or later.

Note

1. Those eleven questions were an exact replica of the characteristics of supervisory behaviour used by Nightingale (1982) in his recent study on workplace democracy in Canada. Contrary to his expectations Nightingale found no significant difference in worker evaluation of supervisory behaviour in the two types of organization, democratic and hierarchical, that he was comparing. Unfortunately, no results of the data analysis were provided in the study report, and thus we have no basis for assessing whether or not the pattern of the evaluation by our respondents is in any way different from that of workers in other workplaces in this country.

Chapter Six
From Quality Control to Quality Assurance

Our research uncovered major differences in interpretation and assumptions between the two methods of quality control used at the Simcoe Bay plant – the American and Japanese. The Japanese approach to achieving quality is very different from the American approach, and failure to understand the differences has resulted in considerable strain on both workers and supervisors at Simcoe Bay. These differences between the two can best be understood by comparing the JME and Arcan approaches to ensuring the quality of the product, and analysing worker reaction to the transition from North American quality control to Japanese-stype quality assurance. Since JME introduced some but not all elements of the approach to achieving quality employed in their Canadian plant, this chapter will also assess the consequences of partial implementation. Our analysis will once again emphasize the importance to the Japanese approach of the fit between automated technology and the design of the management system.

At Arcan, quality control was emphasized more than any other function in the production process (Ch.3). It was based on the traditional American idea and methodology which focused on inspection to ensure that products met predetermined standards for precision, performance, or appearance. Arcan relied on the inspection department to check for and adjust product quality after production, rather than having workers inspect their own work. QC was therefore a distinct function, separate from production.

Inspection began with parts and materials entering the plant. A sample was checked to ensure conformity with specifications. Quality control personnel were experts, people with a thorough knowledge of the standards, who were assigned to each department within the plant. "Quality control used to make routine checks on all operations. [In] some operations you sent finished work to him before it was passed and he would inspect. In other operations it was a percentage check." Also, the quality control department monitored the output from those machines most likely to cause problems. This monitoring system permitted early detection of errors and enabled rapid identification of the source of the problem, whether it was human error or faulty machinery. To assist in accurate identification of the source of error, the product was coded so that the operator responsible could be identified.

When rejects were found, they were shown to the workers so that they would get an understanding of what rejects were, "what they [were] caused from and what they [came] from." QC personnel assisted workers in meeting the standards, and when the specifications changed the "QC personnel let the people know who [were] working in the areas." Members of the quality control department provided an essential link between the technical personnel who established product specifications and the operators who were responsible for ensuring that they did not create rejects.

The Arcan approach to quality control, an approach we will call error detection and error control, emphasized the scrap rate, the percentage of scrap to total production. Keeping the scrap rate below two per cent was the responsibility of the quality control department. As a result, quality was viewed as resulting from conformity with technical standards established by the technicians and communicated to the operators by members of the QC department. Such standards changed relatively infrequently because the market was assumed to be relatively stable. This reduced the need for constant redesign. Well-designed production processes, dealing with not more than a few kinds of components produced over the years, were finely tuned to reduce error but were rarely redesigned.

Upon reorganizing the Simcoe Bay plant, JME eliminated the quality control department and introduced the method of quality control widely used in Japanese manufacturing companies. The responsibility for quality control was placed in the hands of the production department and quality checking was built into operators' jobs. A banner posted in the Simcoe Bay plant proclaims, "Quality is Everybody's Responsibility." The basic ideas behind the slogan are that quality begins with production, that quality is "everyone's problem," and that quality requires a company-wide "habit of improvement." A worker in close contact with a supervisor is expected to assume an important role in improving the quality of products together with the organization of the production process.

Historically, this approach to quality control, which is rather unique to Japanese industries, evolved from the strenuous efforts made by the manufacturing sector to overcome its low and unreliable state of quality control early in its post-war development (Cusumano, 1985: Ch. 6; Cole, 1979: Chs. 5-6). At that time Japanese companies relied heavily on the guidance and advice of American experts based on the assumption that American techniques and management of quality control must be the most advanced. This reliance on and imitation of western techniques was made necessary by the relative absence then of necessary stocks of expertise and financial resources in the Japanese industrial sector. Nonetheless, Japanese firms were quick to master Western techniques, and gradually devised unique solutions of their own to the problems of quality control. Over the next few years Japanese industries substantially expanded and increased their quality control procedures. Quality control shifted from being the prerogative of expert engineers with limited shop experience to being the responsibility of each employee from top management to workers on the shop floor. This technique soon became standard in Japanese industry. Instead of adding layers of inspectors and reliability assurance personnel to detect quality problems, each worker, in concert with his or her supervisor and workmates, was now expected to take responsibility for problem-solving. This entails giving each worker a button to stop the line when substandard products are produced. The active and constant participation of all line workers in the inspection of quality at all stages of production that Japanese companies have developed over the years is one of the "simple and most profound twists to the original ideas propagated by the western experts" (Cole:136). The Japanese approach to quality control increases the discretion of workers and relies on mutual adjustment among workmates and between workers and supervisors to coordinate behaviour. Direct supervision and standardization of work processes become less important coordinating mechanisms.

JME began to implement this Japanese method of quality control immediately upon taking over the Simcoe Bay plant. The company began by reducing the number of middle managers (Ch. 3), something which could only be accompanied by assigning workers greater control over operational decisions. It also decided to reduce the size of the technostructure with less emphasis on standardization of work processes. By simultaneously changing the locus of responsibility for quality control and operational decisions, as well as the methodology for coordinating workers with one another and with their supervisor, the new approach enabled JME to eliminate twenty-six people at Arcan who had been engaged in quality control and additional personnel who had been involved in implementing corrective measures. Reducing the division of labour by assigning responsibility for quality control to work groups permitted the leaner structure characteristic of Japanese manufacturing operations.

JME's introduction of the self-inspection system meant that the excess of personnel in the QC department with Arcan disappeared, and that "nobody [was] standing behind workers to catch the defects any more." A veteran worker on the shop floor has witnessed the change in the practice:

> Quality control people no longer exist with JME. JME relies on the worker to be his own control inspector. He is expected to do the job right. That brings more responsibility to his job. There were a lot of times in the Arcan days where people would say, 'I don't know what we need the QC personnel for. We know how to do the job.'

But self-inspection is only one component in JME's approach to quality. In an attempt to shift from the American type of quality control to JME's way, the focus has been shifted from the "QC way of thinking" to a QA (quality assurance) orientation. Quality assurance is a process employing an open systems perspective. The interface between the production process and the consumer is carefully monitored so that products can be redesigned to increase market penetration. Such monitoring enables the manufacturing firm to adjust their products to changing customer needs and preferences. The goal of such monitoring is not to detect errors so that they can be corrected; rather, the company is monitoring positive and negative feedback so that adjustments can be made in the organization of the production process to reduce customer dissatisfaction while accentuating those characteristics of the products generating satisfaction. Thus, monitoring is not designed to improve customer relations, "to cool out the market." Its purpose is to identify forms of product design that will increase the satisfaction of customers in general, not merely those complaining with the product in the future. It is for this reason that customer returns and the problems which lead to the returns are monitored closely, and that, as discussed in the previous chapter, customer service has become emphasized as the most important function at JME's Canadian operation. JME's emphasis on customer service and on quality assurance are thus tied together: "the two are paired concepts." The Japanese production manager explains:

> QC is a concept laid down for the insiders, that is, within the factory, something you do in the process of making components. Quality assurance, on the other hand, is a function aimed at outsiders. It comes from outsiders, i.e. customers. The feedback from the customers is brought back to the factory for examination and the necessary remedy is provided based on the feedback. We put more emphasis on QA function [than QC] here and would be vigorously pursuing the necessary activities with the aim of reducing the claims from our customer.

The Arcan system sought to reduce defects through error detection and error control – through a process of monitoring to ensure conformity with specifications. The JME approach to reducing defects emphasizes automation and improving the flow of people, materials and product from one sub-process to another. Focusing on the flow among sub-processes stresses the constant need to improve coordination and develop techniques to increase the efficient utilization of scarce resources. Monden (1985:78) terms this process the "smoothing of production." Automation is used when work can be highly standardized to increase the consistency and precision of performance; it is valued because it facilitates consistent quality. Properly designed machines can be more precise and consistent than human beings. Thus, those activities which are governed by stable decision rules based on a small number of known contingencies can be performed by machines. However, as work becomes more complex, increasing the contingencies and the number of feasible options, people rather than machines must perform the tasks. At the same time human operators must act as consistently as machines, keeping conditions standardized, to ensure the steady flows necessary for human, machine and material resources to be fully utilized. JME's production manager further elaborates on this process:

> You can achieve a very high level of quality if every product is made by machine; production and materials are done automatically and operators keep conditions standardized [as a result of engineering design]. There would be no defects if conditions could be highly standardized. Quality control depends on new [automated] machines [which will reduce the amount of handling] and quality depends on being able to operate according to plan.

If management aims to keep conditions standardized without standardizing the way the work is to be done, workers need a thorough understanding of the production process. The depth of that understanding can only be assessed when there is a failure or trouble and workers have to respond. "Then we find out if they [workers] have the theoretical and systematic training needed. If they've understood, they can make repairs," argues the production manager. Thus, under the Japanese system, understanding the production process is the fundamental condition for the effectiveness of the system of quality control. Understanding the production processes, to put it another way, is required, not just desired, so that the sub-processes can be redesigned constantly to improve the degree to which elements of the production process complement one another.

The distinction between this approach and that characterizing Arcan is indeed fundamental:

> In Canada, if something goes wrong, they expect me to tell them whether it's an electrical or mechanical problem so they can assign someone with electrical or someone with

mechanical expertise. You can't separate like that. One person has to be able to make any repairs a given machine might require. The problem is not electrical or mechanical. The problem is to repair the machine.

Stated another way, according to Japanese theory, people should specialize in restoring and improving the integration of a configuration of production processes. They should not specialize in mechanical or electrical problems, but in understanding the interfaces among sets of processes. The most important condition for effective quality control is the ability to constantly redesign and improve the sub-parts comprising the production process, constantly identifying when automation can be used effectively and when refinements to the product can increase customer satisfaction.

In this perspective, redesign is not exclusively the responsibility of an engineer in a far-off laboratory; it is the responsibility of operating personnel who have gained an understanding of the production process through participation in that process. For it is the operating personnel who are most aware of the linkages among production processes and of the weaknesses in their integration. Strengthening the integration among production processes generates improved technology and improves the ability to operate according to plan. The flow of people, goods and materials becomes smoother and pre-planning becomes increasingly effective. As a result, quality increases. Quality is the product of well-designed allocative and coordinating mechanisms. It is achieved by increasing the fit between the structure of the organization and the contingencies that the organization faces. Creating a close fit necessitates a high degree of responsiveness to the dynamic environment within which the organization operates.

Thus, JME's approach to improve quality emphasized redesigning the organization of the production process rather than controlling human and machine error. In the quality assurance perspective, management hoped to introduce a production process that would be continually adjusted to increase the smoothness of the flow and to respond rapidly to customer feedback and changes in the market. As a result of redesign, according to this scenario, specifications are constantly changing and machinery is modified so that there is increasing satisfaction with the organization's output. People are reassigned so that their efforts can complement the production process more effectively; their understanding of that process increases continually.

This at least was the theory behind the system of quality control that JME wanted to adopt. Error detection and error control as emphasized by Arcan were not critical concerns for Japanese management because, in their view, as soon as behaviour can be standardized, it can for the most part be built into the engineering design of a product and into the instrumentation of the production plan and the equipment. A given level of quality, determined by what customers request, is inserted in the engineering design of a product; preventive devices to detect defective work in machines and production lines are also designed. Unfortunately for JME, this built-in mechanism for quality control and perpetual redesign to improve product quality has not been fully operating up to now in the Simcoe Bay plant because attention has so far centred on the introduction of new technologies developed in Japan. The difficulties encountered in creating smooth flows following introduction of large scale new technologies have consumed the energy of employees and directed their attention inwards. But the company believes that it is moving in the direction of "autonomation" (Monden, 1985). As long as employees are moving "in the right direction," quality control is not the "the big issue." This view is reflected in one of the Japanese manager's comments:

> These days quality control is simply a matter of consciousness. When you make things, you would like to do it right and neatly; so your products look good and fine. I don't think it has created any extra work or caused stress on workers, simply because they have to check the quality of their products. All they need is to be a little bit alert and perceptive.

In practice, however, JME has found that this new open system orientation which it has attempted to introduce has been to a large extent misunderstood by its employees, as has its approach to improving quality. This lack of understanding is reflected in worker responses to the open-ended question posed by our questionnaire: "In your view, what are the most important differences between the way work was done at Arcan and the way it is done at JME?" Here is a sample of the answers:

> Quality control at JME is not nearly as good as at Arcan.
> More emphasis was put on quality at Arcan than at JME.
> Arcan stressed more on quality and had manpower.

> Arcan had quality control and JME doesn't believe in it.
>
> No quality control at JME. Workers have too much of a work load to be quality conscious.
>
> JME wants quantity not quality.
>
> Quality is less controlled now at JME.
>
> We don't have enough people to work on American equipment, so we need quality control at JME.
>
> Quality control used by Arcan should be adopted by JME.

A majority of workers are very critical of the JME approach to quality control. To some workers the elimination of the QC department by JME means "no quality control at JME," partly because "JME doesn't believe in quality control." This is in contrast to their perception of Arcan's QC policies. Many respondents maintain that Arcan "had quality control." With enough QC personnel doing "nothing but inspection," quality was well controlled at Arcan. Through the thorough process of inspection in every department "problems were spotted before they got out of control."

Other workers understand that the new method of self-inspection is an expected part of their job, but feel that it has not and cannot be enforced because of the increased workload and the pace of work, or because of the lack of motivation or consciousness among some workers. Obviously, part of the workers' misunderstanding is due to a lack of training; without adequate training to gain full understanding of the process a worker is unable to be "alert and perceptive" all the time.

In responding to the question, "Do you prefer the Arcan or JME approach to quality control and quality assurance?", therefore, sixty-three per cent of those who had worked for Arcan indicated that they preferred the Arcan approach while only one of ten prefers JME's approach. (The rest were either 'don't know' or 'both inadequate.') When asked to elaborate, workers expressed the following concerns about self-inspection:

> I think JME should have quality control. It'd catch a lot. Where I'm working, you don't have time to do quality checking. If we had more time, we could do a better job and probably put out better quality. You've got to do your own

quality control, as you're working. I find it's too hectic to actually do a proper job.

I'm a firm believer that JME should adopt quality control that Arcan had. Where I work, you're the last person to look at the product before it's passed out and shipped out. You've got about 30 things to look at in about 15 seconds. You can't do it. Maybe a robot could, but we can't. You can only go so fast. I don't know how it runs in Japan and how they do that.

I think the Arcan method is a lot more reliable than the machine QC or letting each individual do their own inspection. It's not working out. Before, workers were only here to do a certain job; they did that job, and they were not doing other jobs. The odd one might do inspection, but not all of them for sure. When they had QC personnel doing quality inspection, you had less scrap and there's always somebody responsible for the scrap. The way it is here now, you can go and blame everybody in the whole place. Who's responsible for scrap? You can't operate that way.

A worker off the line summarizes the points made by respondents:

I worked virtually everywhere in the plant at Arcan for 10 years. The Arcan QC approach is better. I think the rejects were caught early in the production. Right now I think there's a lot of waste because if they don't find problems right to the very end, all that amount of work done to the product [is waste] before it's even detected. The JME approach is feasible to a certain extent. There are many things that the average worker wouldn't know, whether it is a reject or not. I think there are a lot of people who wouldn't care one way or the other.

These quotations focus on rejects or scrap rates. The self-inspection and quality assurance systems are deemed by the workers to be less effective than error detection and control as techniques for limiting rejects. This exists because at JME there is a scrap rate greater than the two per cent deemed acceptable by Arcan. This higher percentage of scrap has also led many workers to assume that fellow workers are not adequately concerned with quality:

At JME, they want quality, but they depend on the individual. That's fine if everybody is really dedicated. But you don't get everybody dedicated. You have 10 people and maybe five of them are and the other five aren't; so it's very hard to go by quality that way. I think they should bring QC back.

> They put in every man's responsible for his work, but a lot of the guys don't care about it. They haven't got the education to know what they're supposed to be doing properly. They haven't been trained. In the Arcan way there was one guy who knew exactly what the specs [specifications] were on everything. I thought that was better.

Explanations for the high scrap rates emphasize lack of education, lack of training, lack of dedication, too little time, too many tasks, too much delay in identifying problems and too little expertise. Given these problems the traditional Arcan approaches to production – closer supervision of workers, narrow job definitions, and greater standardization of work processes – are deemed necessary, according to some respondents, "if we're not going to put a lot of junk in the parking lot."

> Here [at JME] you get the feeling they don't care what the finished result is as long as they've got the numbers. We seem to be producing an awful lot of scrap and it doesn't seem to be worrying anybody. Arcan was more concerned with keeping scrap down so you were required to do a little better job. You concentrated on what you were doing.

Quality control was indeed a pressing issue for workers while our research was being carried out, because in the summer of 1986 large amounts of scrap were piled at the end of the employee parking lot. Piles of rejected items were viewed by employees as an indication of the company's failure to generate a quality product. Given the quantity of scrap most employees felt that the company was unlikely to stay in business since too little profit would be generated under such circumstances. It should be noted here that the performance standard for plant operations that the workers were using was the acceptable scrap rate, rather than success in improving the integration of flows making up the production process. In other words, workers did not understand that JME's performance standards differ from Arcan's. Because of the levels of scrap generated, they saw JME as unconcerned about the quality of work. The quotations cited above suggest that they believed JME's concern with quality was secondary to the priority placed on quantity – the targeted amount of production.

Our questionnaire provides other data which shed more light on worker perceptions and assessments of the issue of quality control at their workplace. These emerged from the question comparing work practices at JME and at Arcan. This question listed eleven items to be considered: five of the eleven concerned themselves with work practices in relation to quality of work. The question was identical to the one that was raised in the White and Trevor study in Great Britain, and this allowed us to compare the results from the two national sample groups. Employees at the Simcoe Bay plant were asked to rate the degree of importance placed on various aspects of work organization in practice both at JME (all employees) and at Arcan (only ex-Arcan employees). The results (Table 6.1) were consistent with the pattern which emerged from the interviews quoted above.

Table 6.1:   Perceptions of Working Practices: JME and Arcan

Working Practices	JME (all employees)	Arcan (only ex-Arcan employees)
Thoroughness of planning	3.1	2.4
Efficiency with which work is organized	3.1	2.4
Concern with quality of work	2.9	1.9
Concern with quality of service	2.8	2.1
Amount of checking and double checking	3.4	2.0
Own time spent on checking	2.9	2.3
Work checked by others	3.3	2.0
Emphasis on rules and procedures	2.6	2.5
Strictness about mistakes	3.0	2.5
Strictness about discipline, e.g. timekeeping	2.6	2.5
Management's interest in details of work	3.2	2.4

Based on scores from questions using a 5-point scale with 1 = very important, 5 = very unimportant. Thus the higher the score the less important a practice is deemed to be.

Whether quality is seen in terms of the quality of work in general or of service given to customers, ex-Arcan employees perceive Arcan as having been more persistent and proficient. JME, on the other hand, is viewed as less concerned about the quality of work, the level of the concern being lower than the median (close to a three in a five-point rating scale). Ex-Arcan employees perceive that Arcan placed more emphasis on 'checking and double-checking' than does JME; while JME uses the method of self-inspection rather than 'detailed checking by someone else' as the means of achieving quality. These figures suggest that while workers are aware of the practice of self-inspection endorsed by the management, they consider it to be less effective in ensuring that problems are detected and eliminated early in the process.

The differences in workers' perceptions between the two Japanese-owned and managed manufacturing firms, JME in Canada and Company A in Britain, are rather striking (Table 6.2). White and Trevor found that British workers identified the Japanese approach to quality as the most distinctive difference between the Japanese-owned companies for which they now worked and other companies for which they had previously worked. British workers consistently saw their Japanese employers as assigning the highest priority to quality standards: "the company is very, very, very quality conscious" (White and Trevor:64) or "the company would never compromise over quality" (32). At Company B, another Japanese firm investigated by White and Trevor, the majority of the workers saw the checking of work as part of their own responsibility; though some of them saw this responsibility as, at least initially, a taxing one (64). The British finding was that both managers and workers employed by the Japanese companies were in no doubt that the quality control system at their company was exceptionally effective.

Our data are contrary to the British findings; workers at the Simcoe Bay plant have some serious doubts about the efficacy of their company's quality control system. It is quite likely that the costs associated with the piecemeal adoption of automated machinery as opposed to a large scale, integrated introduction has led to greater worker concern with the effectiveness of new methodologies, including the quality control method. The response of three populations to working practices supports this interpretation. The three populations are JME workers with previous experience at Arcan, JME workers who were not previously employed by

Arcan, and British workers in a Japanese branch plant, Company A, which had been unconstrained in the introduction of Japanese management.

Table 6.2: Perceptions of Working Practices: Experienced and Inexperienced Workers in Japanese-Managed Plants in Canada and Great Britain

Working Practices	JME Canada		Company A Great Britain*
	Experienced: Ex-Arcan Employees	Inex-perienced	Inex-perienced
Thoroughness of planning	3.2	2.5	1.8
Efficiency with which work organized	3.2	2.3	1.5
Concern with quality of work	3.0	1.9	1.2
Concern with quality of service	2.9	2.0	1.2
Amount of checking and double checking	3.6	2.2	1.4
Own time spent on checking	3.0	2.2	2.9
Work checked by others	3.4	2.6	3.3
Emphasis on rules and procedures	2.7	2.0	1.3
Strictness about mistakes	3.0	2.6	2.3
Strictness about discipline, e.g. timekeeping	2.6	2.2	1.5
Management's interest in details of work	3.3	2.4	1.6

*Source: White, Michael and Trevor, Malcom, *Under Japanese Management*, p. 33

Company A, which was investigated by the British researchers, was unconstrained in the introduction of their management because they were able to establish it in the 'greenfield.' The Japanese designed their own plant, work practices and machinery to complement their own way of doing business. The organizational structures of the plant were likewise constructed so that they were consistent with the company's working practices. Workers were young, much younger than ex-employees of Arcan at JME, and better qualified. Most of them received their training and socialization from the Japanese employer rather than from a previous employer. Likewise, as noted earlier in this report, those employees who were recruited by JME in Simcoe Bay tend to be young and better educated than the rest of the work force (Ch. 2).

Respondents with no previous work experience with Arcan, those recruited by JME, more closely approximate the perceptions of working practices held by the British workers.[1] These data suggest the interactive effect of the experience of workers and the consequences of constrained or unconstrained introduction of Japanese management. When workers are inexperienced and introduction is unconstrained, then working practices in a Japanese-owned factory are more likely to be perceived as distinctive and positively evaluated. On the other hand, when workers are experienced and the introduction of the configuration of practices comprising the Japanese approach to quality remains incomplete, Japanese working practices are less positively evaluated. This conclusion is reinforced by the fact that former Arcan employees at JME perceive the Japanese approach as unsystematic, decision-making as ad hoc rather than comprehensive, and coordinating mechanisms as less rather than more effective.

Therefore, the data presented and the differences described in this section are sufficiently great and coherent to suggest that workers at JME lack an understanding of the differences in assumptions underlying the American and Japanese approaches to quality control as outlined at the beginning of this chapter. Scrap represented failure at Arcan, and thus workers continue to use the scrap rate to measure performance. According to this particular standard, JME's performance is less acceptable than Arcan's. Japanese managers admit that the level of rejects at JME is high, much higher than at their home plant. However, they consider the scrap rate to be "not so abnormal" given the fact that new machinery is being introduced, and the smoothing process is far from complete. The workers, however, have not been told that temporarily high rates should be expected.

However, the lower scrap rate at Arcan does not mean there were no rejected items. In his comparison of QC methods in U.S. and Japanese auto manufacturing firms, Cole (1979:136) noted that there are in fact a large number of rejected items in American firms that need to be repaired before they can be further processed. In the case of the Ford Motor Company, the repair average was about ten per cent. Ten per cent of labour was engaged in repairing items that did not meet specifications. The emphasis placed on repairing can be seen, Cole maintained, from the large number of quality inspectors constantly on the job. At Arcan, as well, repair-salvage was one of the most vigorously pursued activities and was regarded as an important part of production. Normally, twenty to twenty-five workers on the floor per shift (approximately 10 per cent of the production work force) were assigned specifically to perform the repair-salvage tasks. Salvage was an integral part of production, and thus manufacturing and salvage were conducted at the same time as part of the same process.

Rejected items at JME look large because they are left unrepaired. JME management does not view salvage as an integral part of the production process. The reason is that the Japanese do not use salvage as a diagnostic tool – a way of identifying sources of error which can be corrected. Instead, Japanese managers believe that salvage is a completely separate process and that the resources devoted to salvage should depend on the profitability to be realized, which is largely dependent on the market for materials salvaged. For these managers, scrap rates are not then an indicator of success (or failure as seen by some employees) and salvaging rejected items is a relatively low priority except when it becomes profitable and the work force becomes available to undertake that activity. Japanese management would normally sell scrap to other firms for reprocessing. However, in Simcoe Bay no firm as yet exists that could undertake this function.

Instead of focusing on examining and reworking rejected items, Japanese managers with their QA orientation measure the ratio of output with which customers are satisfied to the number of employees. The quantity of products with which customers are satisfied is their measure of the success they have achieved in coordinating work processes. They view quality as resulting when a "smoothing production" is maintained at a satisfactory level so that the targeted number of products is achieved. For them quality and quantity are two inseparable concepts, and should come together. The level of quality is considered satisfactory when customer needs are understood and met and the processes for meeting those needs are effectively coordinated. The emphasis is thus on coordination among production processes and not on correcting errors.

These assumptions, however, have not been communicated to JME's employees, many of whom believe that considerable unnecessary waste is occurring because components which could be repaired and which would have been repaired under Arcan are not being repaired:

> We used to have a salvage department before. ....They'd rework the scrap, take it apart, save the parts. JME management didn't believe in a salvage department.

> It makes you mad when you see all this expensive stuff just going in the garbage.

> There's a million dollars worth of scrap out there in the parking lot. I don't believe in that. Arcan would never have let that kind of money go down the product. [sic]

In the eyes of the employees, repair and salvage are being neglected because the company is more concerned with quantity than quality and because the company is understaffed and is thus diverting personnel from repair/salvage to other operations. The employees believe that management's priorities are inappropriate and its policies short-sighted and wasteful. In comparison, then, Arcan's approach to quality is seen as preferable.

When JME reopened the Simcoe Bay plant, indoctrination was employed to promote the idea that quality begins with production, quality is "everybody's problem" and quality requires a company-wide "habit of improvement." No effort was made, however, to identify for employees the ways in which the JME approach to improving quality differed from Arcan's approach. Employees were not introduced to the ideas and assumptions of "total quality control" adopted by JME. As a result, the nature and magnitude of the differences between the two were underestimated by both supervisors and workers; creating improved quality was treated as a motivational rather than an organizational problem by management. The consequence has been to have a mixture of the traditional North American approach and the new Japanese idea in use to increasing quality.

Furthermore, since management initially assumed that operators were pre-trained (as an average they have a ten-year tenure in the job of making components), no effort was made to re-train them. Failure to explain differences in American and Japanese assumptions and interpretations led supervisors and workers to stress error detection rather than improving the smoothness of work flows. Workers seem to believe that rejected items should be analyzed as Arcan did, so that controls needed to reduce error can be developed and imposed. Their views, inherited from Arcan, are that production processes should be improved by improving the understanding of what can go wrong.

Japanese management at JME operates by a set of assumptions that might seem strange to workers but that contribute to its overall success. Similarly, workers continue to operate by a set of assumptions and principles learned from Arcan, their former employer. While these may seem outdated and inadequate to Japanese managers, in the eyes of the workers these practices contribute to achieving lower scrap rates and bringing in "the best quality products."

Many employees at JME have not hidden their resistance to change in one way or other and some have openly expressed their preference for the way things used to be done, simply because differences in underlying assumptions have never communicated or understood. The concerns revealed by employees on the floor are due in part to their response to the transition to a highly computerized production system which is largely new to them, and in part to the lack of explanations of why and how the new system should be employed. Restructuring the production system under JME has been done piecemeal, and it is an ongoing process. The piecemeal implementation of change has reduced the degree of consistency among design parameters of the organization. As a result, the integration of the configurations of processes comprising Japanese management has been reduced. With reduced integration, it follows that employees have a less complete understanding of the ways in which the assumptions of Japanese management differ from those of American management. Delays in introducing high degrees of automation have accentuated this problem. To get large-scale automated machinery to operate effectively requires a lengthy period of time and depends on the support from the head office, both technical and financial. The length of time that this transition has taken so far and the amount of scrap produced during this transition have reduced satisfaction with the JME approach and increased the sense among workers that Arcan's approach would have been less costly.

JME's approach to quality control could only have been effective if the Simcoe Bay plant had been completely reorganized. Japanese quality control requires a flexible structure rather than the mechanical bureaucracy employed by Arcan. An ongoing redesign process is not possible when thinking and doing are segregated from one another and flows are tightly regulated (Mintzberg). JME's transition to a more flexible structure has at best been partial and both operators and managers continue to define thinking as a managerial responsibility and to believe that managers alone are responsible for redesigning the subparts of the production process. Essential changes in structure and assumptions have thus not occurred.

A strategy and policy on the part of management for dealing with change for the forthcoming period seems of critical importance. Change in the approach to quality is just one aspect of the production process and the company needs to have a comprehensive plan for transforming production management. As one respondent noted, "QC can't be the same [under the new system] because of automation." What management can do in the meantime may be, as another respondent suggested, to hold an intensive reorientation session for everybody involved in the operation, including operators. In that kind of session, some fundamental principles and assumptions of the production system can be debated and discussed. This could be the beginning of a new commitment on the part of management to helping workers understand the production process, which is the fundamental condition for the effectiveness of the whole system, including the system of ts quality control.

Note

1. In interpreting these data, it is important to remember that data for JME's experienced workers are likely to be more valid than in either of the other cases since all workers questioned were comparing JME with Arcan, two companies engaged in the same form of production. Inexperienced workers are comparing Japanese management either with the practices of a variety of other companies or with expectations of what companies might be like.

Chapter Seven
Worker Search for Security and Job Satisfaction

One of the major findings of White and Trevor's study in Great Britain was that workers under Japanese management were not more satisfied with their employment than those in comparable non-Japanese companies. The study provided little support for the notion that Japanese practice depends on creating particularly 'happy' or 'contented' workers, or on generating particularly strong feelings among workers that human relations in the company are a high priority. The companies were not attempting to win worker loyalty and commitment by fostering exceptionally high levels of satisfaction with employment. Nonetheless, Japanese manufacturing firms operating in Europe have been reported to be achieving high levels of labour productivity and product quality (Takamiya, 1981; White and Trevor, 1983). The Japanese advantage, White and Trevor argued, lies in the organization of work and in British workers' acceptance of the work methods used and the competence of management at Japanese firms.

Unlike the British case, however, at JME in Simcoe Bay there is very little evidence to indicate worker acceptance either of the work methods used by the new management or of the competence of that management. This has been particularly evident in the debate on quality control methods reviewed in the previous chapter. It is thus not surprising to find that Canadian workers under JME are somewhat less satisfied with their employment than were those in Great Britain. Workers' ratings of their own satisfaction or dissatisfaction with various aspects of their employment at JME and in Great Britain are presented in the average scores in Table 7.1 (the comparison was made possible because the questions used in the British study were duplicated in our questionnaire survey). It is not legitimate, as noted by the British researchers, to conclude that people are more satisfied with one aspect of their job than with another because criteria of evaluation may shift from one question to another. It is possible, however, to compare the average scores for different groups of respondents on the same question.

The evidence provided by previous studies conducted in the field of industrial sociology reveals that the large majority of workers, if asked how they like their jobs, tend to give generally favourable answers, or, if asked to rate the level of their satisfaction on some sort of scale, tend to make choices which fall in the positive range. A Canadian survey by Burnstein, et al., (1975) for the Economic Council of Canada, for example, reports that forty per cent of respondents are 'very satisfied' with their jobs and fully eighty-nine per cent of Canadians are at least 'somewhat satisfied' with their jobs.

For the thirteen questions asked, responses of the sample group of workers at JME averaged 3.0 on a six-point scale. The reported levels of job satisfaction must be interpreted with caution, but it is true that people tended not to give favourable answers. JME can even be depicted as a factory in which employees are on the whole rather dissatisfied or unhappy with their employment.

It cannot be denied that the general dissatisfaction of workers with their jobs stems from basic, inherent features of the "line work" – repetitiveness, monotony, and mechanical pacing. This is not unique to workers at JME. The majority of workers at the plant who happen to be semi-skilled operators can be expected to gain little direct reward from their jobs. "It is factory work; it is just a job; this job gives me a pay cheque, not satisfaction." However, beyond the dislike of factory work, this dissatisfaction among JME employees seems to be derived from several factors peculiar to the conditions under which the Simcoe Bay plant was operating at the time the survey was conducted.

Table 7.1: Average Job Satisfaction Ratings: Canada and Great Britain

Satisfaction	Canada JME (N=267)	Great Britain[*]	
		Company A (N=146)	Company B[**] (N=28)
How you get on with management	2.7	2.7	2.9
The security of the job	3.0	1.9	2.3
How worthwhile the job is	2.7	2.5	2.3
How interesting the job is	2.7	2.6	2.5
Fringe benefits like pensions and sick pay	2.5	3.5	4.1
The friendliness of people you work with	2.1	2.2	1.8
Hours of work (including travel)	2.9	2.8	2.6
The opportunity to get on with your work in your own way	2.8	2.4	2.3
Your pay	3.2	2.8	2.6
Your working conditions	3.4	2.5	2.5
Training	3.5	2.8	3.4
Promotion chances	3.9	3.1	3.1
Trade union strength	3.4	-	-

Based on a 6-point rating scale with 1= completely satisfied, 6= completely dissatisfied.

[*]White and Trevor, *Under Japanese Management*, Table 3:12, 5:3

[**]Company B is Japanese-owned but managed by local British managers and thus regarded as less 'Japanese' by White and Trevor.

Work pressure is one of the factors. Some workers on the shop floor feel under high pressure to turn out work in quantity. The pace of work is, in any case, fixed by the process, and has not necessarily been increased to a noticeable degree. But as it becomes more and more automated with the new lines introduced by JME, the pace of work is felt to be faster and the pressure to "produce more" was felt to be greater than it used to be largely because of the tightness of staffing levels in production. More than half of those expressing some sort of dissatisfaction have made reference to the magnitude of staff reductions. These people almost always connect tightness of staffing levels with broader responsibilities, for example, inspection of the quality of products assigned to them under the new management. One female operator expresses her feelings about the increased pace in her work due to the reduction of staffing:

> I'm physically tired when I go home by the amount of work. The machine runs every x seconds. They slapped coding on us and extra inspection things, and they keep putting more on us, and don't give us any more time to do the job. If there is a fluke, they come back at us and there's your code on the cap so that you get in trouble. I don't think that is fair. They should get it straight and allow a period so you can do the job and do it properly. There's no way you can do it like this.

Some other workers are reluctant to accept the intense work demands on their lives, emphasizing the physical intensity and difficulty of their jobs. Another female worker is uneasy about her job because of its physical demands:

> As women, we are handling a tremendous amount of weight. It's a slugging job and I feel as if it's more than our capacity. It's way too much. How long can I keep it up? I'll go and look for a better job if I feel the situation is the way I want with more appropriate hours and not so heavy work. I don't intend to retire here. By all means.

These people seem frustrated by the work load. There are "bad feelings" about the intensity of it as the production has started to rise. Some of the jobs are indeed too difficult, too physically demanding, one of the supervisors commented. He emphasized that some workers, notably women who are doing heavy lifting, are having a hard time because of the physical demands in some of the jobs, particularly if "you have to do it day after day." With the lax pace of work with Arcan, explained the supervisor, workers who used to work for "half-on and half-off" have found it especially painful to adjust to the steadiness in work flow, which is persistently emphasized as important by the new management.

Workers at any place of employment need to be appreciated for the work they do. Some workers at JME feel dissatisfied and discontented because they perceive themselves to be less appreciated and rewarded for their efforts by the new management. In the view of one male worker the company does not show any concern for people, and this has led to his frustration and dissatisfaction with his employment:

> With Arcan I enjoyed coming to work. But I'm finding with this one it's less and less enjoyment. I don't know why. I appreciate being thanked for my work, and I think every human does too. You're not thanked here. It doesn't matter. Weekends you give a little extra, but no appreciation for that. With Arcan a lot of foremen would come over and thank you.

The employees at JME rate themselves considerably less satisfied than their counterparts in Britain, particularly in terms of job security, pay, and working conditions on the job (Table 7.1). The only marked advantage which JME employees seem to enjoy is in regard to fringe benefits; although JME does not offer anything exceptional in this respect. JME took over the benefit package formulated between the union and Arcan in its complete form. No additional provisions were introduced at all. It was regarded as competitive with other large firms in the area and generally perceived favourably by employees. No complaints or grievances have been heard in this respect.

In the remaining areas of employment, the results are not greatly dissimilar to those obtained from British employees at the two Japanese-owned and managed companies, Company A and B, respectively, as shown in Table 7.1. Yet overall, there is a significantly lower level of satisfaction, particularly for the ex-Arcan employees, in almost every aspect of their employment at JME (Table 7.2). The level of satisfaction among workers newly employed by JME with no experience with the former employer is closer to that of the British workers. These new employees demonstrate a significantly higher level of satisfaction in regard to pay, job security and working conditions than do ex-Arcan employees.

Table 7.2: Average Job Satisfaction Ratings: JME

	JME	
	Ex-Arcan Employees (N=208)	New Employees (N=33)
How you get on with management	2.8	2.3
The security of the job	3.0	2.7
How worthwhile the job is	2.7	2.7
How interesting the job is	2.7	2.6
Fringe benefits like pensions and sick pay	2.3	2.8
The friendliness of people you work with	2.2	2.1
Hours of work (including travel)	3.0	2.4
The opportunity to get on with your work in your own way	2.8	2.8
Your pay	3.3	2.6
Your working conditions	3.5	2.9
Training	3.6	3.0
Promotion chances	4.0	3.7
Trade union strength	3.4	3.1

Pay, job security, and working conditions in employment are rated as least satisfactory by Canadian workers, while the very same conditions were most favourably rated and perceived as the greatest 'advantages' by British workers at Company A in particular (Table 7.3). This company was identified as the most 'Japanese' company by the researchers. British workers at Company A were asked which features of employment in the company, in comparison with two other employers in the community, were considered to be advantages of working there. The greatest advantages cited by more than fifty per cent of responding employees were job security (eighty-nine per cent), pay (seventy-one per cent) and working conditions (sixty per cent). White and Trevor noted that this exceptionally high degree of satisfaction at Company A in the security of employment was the most distinctive aspect of the company.

Table 7.3: Evaluation of Employers: JME, Canada and Company A, Great Britain

	Company A* % Selecting each 'Advantage'	JME % Selecting each 'Above average'
Type of management	50	11
Nature of the work	39	15
Security of jobs	89	27
Money you can earn	71	25
Hours of shifts	23	12
Working conditions	60	12
Chance of promotion or of getting onto a better job	39	9
Opportunity to learn or use skills	39	17

*White and Trevor, *Under Japanese Management*, Table 3.10 p. 30

The results from the British study indicate that, in the case of British workers at the Japanese firm, workers' commitment to their company depended on their assessment of employment security and of the company's ability to pay high wages, coupled with good prospects for promotion, as well as their general satisfaction with working conditions. The particularly high proportion of employees selecting job security as a reason for their attachment to Company A is in sharp contrast to the attitude revealed by the Canadian employees. In a slightly differently phrased question, employees at JME were asked to rate features of employment of JME as above or below average. Only twenty-seven per cent rate job security at JME as above average in contrast to nearly ninety per cent of British workers who saw this same feature of employment at their company as a major advantage. Unlike British workers, JME workers show a high degree of dissatisfaction with wages and opportunities for promotion, and with working conditions. How can these differences be explained?

One major difference between Company A in Great Britain and JME in Simcoe Bay is that Company A created a job structure which is closer to the one usually in use in companies in Japan. Under this system jobs are graded in such a way that the pay structure and linkages among jobs within the company provide workers with an opportunity to move to progressively more worthy work – jobs with more challenge, more security, more prestige and better pay. This structure is based on the concept that workers can fashion a career for themselves on the shop floor.

Having inherited the organization of human resources already establishd within Arcan, the JME approach to the organization of human resources has been a piecemeal one, as we elaborated earlier in this report. After some strenuous negotiation with the union, the new company managed to broaden the job classifications, bringing them closer to the Japanese model; yet this has resulted in fact in reducing, instead of expanding, the scope of the promotion ladder. It is now truncated further than it was at Arcan because the total number of jobs, including quality control positions, has been reduced by half. While the number of jobs has indeed been reduced, existing jobs are still classified into categories which are then linked to different wage rates. This scaled-down version of a basically traditional structure created by Arcan gives workers a vision of limited opportunities for better jobs and higher wages.

Mechanisms for increasing opportunities to think and to influence decisions had been absent under the Arcan operation, and the continued absence reduces the opportunities for gaining a sense that one's work is becoming more worthy even if one is not being promoted. At JME there seems to be no opportunity in sight to increase the worthiness of one's work. The organization of human resources is an integral part of the Japanese model of production (Shimada and MacDuffie, 1987), of which the job structure is the basis for sustaining the organization. Dimensions of "human resource effectiveness" involving job structure, training, reward systems and participation, as Shimada and MacDuffie argue, have to be in place as a complete package in order to be effective in managing human elements in production management. The technical side of the Japanese model of production can be said to have been emphasized by JME at the expense of the human side of the model. The piecemeal introduction of the JME model and the consequences can be seen rather clearly in the issue of job security.

Employees at JME do not rate themselves satisfied with their job security; nonetheless, jobs at JME can be regarded as exceptionally secure by local standards due to the firm, if unusual, commitment to job security that the company made in writing. JME, at the outset, announced that it would keep a regular work force of about five hundred employees at the plant by avoiding layoffs, the provision not being a consequence of its marketing and business policies, but rather a part of its personnel policy. In the 1985 labour contract, the first contract that the company signed with the union, management confirmed its commitment to the work force already hired by endorsing the agreement that "every effort shall be made to avoid layoffs, and regular levels of crewing should be maintained" (Article 28).With that kind of commitment, coupled with the high seniority the majority of employees had earned and retained from their years with Arcan, it is quite clear, in the words of those ex-Arcan employees being interviewed, that their jobs are, generally speaking, "pretty secure."

We've been told more or less that we have a job for life here. That's JME's philosophy sort of thing.

JME is not going to say, 'Oh, forget it,' and sell it and move out. They're bound and determined they're going to make it work.

JME is very unlikely to lay me off.

JME wouldn't lay workers off if they didn't have to.

I'd say something would have to go really wrong for them to shut the plant down. I'd say the job is pretty secure here.

I feel jobs are secure as long as the plant is open, because I'm not a bad worker.

I think my job is pretty secure for as long as I want to work.

These confident words, however, mark the rather complex feelings and views held by the employees which are reflected in the low rating given to job security. These feelings have been compounded by a variety of situations they experienced, beginning with their lay-off by Arcan. After long years of service with Arcan, most workers felt that their jobs with that company were pretty secure, assuming that "the company was going to stay." Arcan's business was perceived as "all right" or "doing well" in workers' minds insofar as they thought they were producing quality products: "Nobody told us anything different." However, as the majority of employees admitted, they were generally not well informed as to what was happening at the company, and the company did not give workers any warning when it decided to close the doors. One day, all of a sudden "the whole thing at Arcan did fall out of components." "They were not interested in making components any more." The plant closing was thus viewed as having resulted from factors beyond the control of the employees, or at least not because of the quality or order problem in the operation. (The issue of the plant closing is discussed in the following chapter of this report.)

Being unemployed for more than a year between the closure by Arcan and the reopening of the plant by JME in the midst of the recession, many people came to realize that there were not many jobs available in the Simcoe Bay area. The area has been known for its high unemployment rate for some time; it has always been higher than the provincial average. Employees in the sample have had a fair amount of direct experience with economic insecurity. Being laid off from Arcan was "the biggest blow" of all for most of them, but still thirty-two per cent of the respondents reported that they had been out of a job for some appreciable length of time previously in their working lives. Thus, there is good reason to feel great anxiety about their basic security in the future.

This anxiety has been compounded by what they see as a number of possible problems under the new JME management. Several respondents pointed to JME's scrap rate as one cause for anxiety: "How much longer can the company operate like this?" They seem to feel that the company is indeed in danger unless it can complete the process of technological restructuring soon and smoothly. They seem not to be assured by the firm's present record in conducting business, including their way of handling matters in industrial relations. Being inexperienced in working with the union under the North American labour-management relations system, Japanese management, they feel, may continue to have "unpleasant relations" with the local union. Thus, at least one worker suggested that it will not be surprising if some day the Japanese pack up and leave. Under the circumstances, several workers were more than a little skeptical about the security of their jobs.

> Job security is an absolute 'must' in the world. But if this place were to close down tomorrow, I wouldn't lose my cool that they closed down and went back to Japan. I can go out and get another job. I'm a sole breadwinner and have family to support; so I do the factory work.

> I can't see them [JME] coming in, spending money – how much? I don't know, to get it going and then turning around and saying the hell with it. But if they do, that will be a business decision.

Increased automation is another factor which gives workers some anxiety about job security. If, as JME's management claims, automation continues to increase in an ongoing way, employees at the operator's level – the majority of the work force – seem to have good reason to be concerned about their job security. Management maintains that any change in technology, including automation, is not going to cost jobs, at least jobs for those already hired, but for many workers such a pronouncement makes little sense. In their view, with the coming of automation the company will not be able to avoid reducing the work force considerably. Some of the older workers also suspect that the company prefers younger workers who will fit in better with the new type of technology, and would like to get rid of long-term employees. Here again words of commitment declared by management in this regard, either officially or unofficially, are not accepted at face value. Workers are worried that management will gradually erode the privileges of worker seniority as well as the company's no-lay-off policy. This is a serious concern, since for many the security of their jobs lies chiefly in the seniority that they have earned over the years in their employment at the plant. Seniority has been "a goal to shoot for" for many of them. These worries were expressed in a number of interviews:

> I think they'll lay off if they keep automation, because they won't be able to keep all the people they have now. They might try to avoid lay-offs, but still they can do so if they want to. They're not going to have a bunch of people standing around a machine not doing anything. I suspect there'll be lay-offs in the next couple of years.

> Robots are coming in like crazy. There's a robot which welds clips and there are two involved in spraying. The new testing line is now highly automated. They are going to connect the lines so that there is less handling. Fewer people will be needed.

Uncertainty due not only to changing technology but also to market fluctuations is the nature of the industry, and employees have learned to live with it. And Arcan used lay-offs regularly to control the work force. JME's management almost did the same in the spring of 1986. Faced with an anticipated decline in demand, management proposed a four-day work week under the government-sponsored work sharing scheme to distribute the incidence of lay-offs. The proposed scheme involved both the salaried and the hourly employees so that the pain could be shared by the plant as a whole. The union opposed the procedures. Fortunately the market turned around quickly enough so that work sharing was not needed. Some, but certainly not all, employees perceived the proposal as a genuine effort by management to prevent lay-offs and keep the regular work force. Such a view nonetheless was not strongly voiced among employees. Even the union executives insisted on the use of a seniority-based lay-off system to respect workers' rights of seniority.

All the above factors have noticeably affected employees' responses to the question: "How likely is it that JME will lay-off workers in the future?" While about thirty-two per cent feel that lay-offs are "very unlikely," an almost equal number, thirty-one per cent feel that they are "somewhat likely." Another thirteen per cent go even further, asserting that they are "very likely," while twenty-four per cent say that they "don't know." These figures are in sharp contrast to other studies done earlier in the field.

The Affluent Worker, for instance, found that ninety per cent of the men studied regarded their jobs as being either 'dead safe' or 'fairly safe' (Goldthorpe, et al., 1968:118). In contrast, less than one-third of workers at JME shared the sense of security common among the British workers decades ago. (With the absence of similar statistics recently gathered in this country, it cannot be fairly assessed how different the above figures of JME workers are from others in the manufacturing industry or any other industry for that matter.) While forty-four per cent of former Arcan employees with higher levels of seniority have indicated that JME is unlikely to lay off workers leaving them temporarily unemployed, six out of ten of those newly employed workers with little seniority seem to believe that lay-offs are somewhat likely (Table 7.4).

Table 7.4: Views about Likelihood of Lay-offs at JME*

Lay-offs	JME Ex-Arcan Employees	New Employees
Very unlikely	43.3%	27.3%
Somewhat likely	38.9	59.1
Very likely	17.8	13.6
	100.0	100.0
	(N = 180)	(N = 22)

* Excluding those whose response to the question is "Don't Know"

Neither the company nor the employees ever explicitly mentioned the idea of lifetime employment as such at the Simcoe Bay plant; yet it is not an unrealistic goal for some workers. Their jobs at the plant could be "for life." Eighteen per cent of respondents in the sample were fifty years of age and over, and for this age group the likelihood of being a lifetime employee is quite high. Many of the remaining employees also seem to have few doubts about remaining at the plant for a long time, if not until retirement, "as long as the company keeps its operation and components are made."

It is a commonly accepted fact that as workers grow older, they are less able to move around and so become more dependent on company benefits. Thus, for most of the workers at JME, the idea of moving to another job, in spite of the relatively low level of satisfaction with their employment overall, is not a feasible or a likely one. Unlike British workers studied by White and Trevor, these employees are not open-minded about the idea. When they were asked what they thought was the best way to get ahead, the large majority of employees at JME answered that the best way was to stay with the present firm, as compared with forty-six per cent of British workers at Company A and twenty-three per cent at other British firms cited in the White and Trevor study (Table 7.5). These differences are largely due to the age difference between the groups. At Company A about two-thirds of employees were under twenty-five years of age; whereas slightly less than ten per cent of the work force at JME is that young.

The evidence that six out of ten employees at JME maintain that they would be better off not moving seems quite contrary to the North American habit of job mobility. This may surprise Japanese managers whose vision of North American workers is that they are constantly on the move. Job mobility appears to be out of the question for most of the people at JME in Simcoe Bay where there are no other jobs known to be available which offer sufficiently greater rewards, financial or otherwise, to make a move worthwhile. Most workers wish to remain at the plant permanently (although a question was not posed specifically to prove this in our survey investigation).

Table 7.5: Views about Changing Jobs: Canada and Great Britain

The best way to get a better job	Canada JME	Great Britain* Company A	British Firm
Stay with the same firm	56%	46%	23%
Move around	10	7	14
It depends (both equally)	6	44	16
Don't know	26	3	4
	100 (N=266)	100 (N= 146)	100 (N= 92)

Are you thinking of changing jobs?

Yes	13%	21%	21%
No	49	66	72
Not sure (weighing possibility)	22	12	7
Don't know	16	0	0
	100 (N= 266)	100 (N= 146)	100 (N= 92)

* White and Trevor, *Under Japanese Management*, Table 3.6, p. 26

Thus, only thirteen per cent of those workers who responded were actively thinking of changing jobs at the time of the interview, the proportion being considerably smaller than their British counterparts. On being asked whether or not they were thinking of changing jobs in the near future, a fair proportion of the respondents said that they were weighing the possibility. Combining these respondents with those who said 'don't know' and 'not sure,' nearly forty per cent of workers were not really thinking about leaving, and were not seriously searching for another job. This high degree of attachment by the respondents to the firm, which is also shown in low levels of labour turnover, is demonstrated despite the questionnaire findings that their work affords no high degree of immediate satisfaction. Those who reported that the work pace was too fast or the work load was excessive and overwhelming, were not more likely than others in the sample to be considering the possibility of taking employment with some other firm. This finding reinforces the conclusion that Goldthorpe, et al. (1968:31-32) drew from their findings: workers' experience of their immediate work-task and roles cannot be associated in any direct way with job satisfaction in terms of workers' attachment to their present employment. The researchers in *The Affluent Worker* summed this up as follows:

> The degree of the attachment is determined by a number of factors of which the nature of work-tasks and -roles are but one. Work which by its very nature entails severe deprivations for those who perform it may nonetheless offer extrinsic – that is, economic – rewards which are such as to attach workers fairly firmly to the employer who offers this work.

Worker attachment or commitment to their company thus largely depends on the company's ability to pay higher wages and to offer security of employment, which is commonly rated among the most important job characteristics by industrial workers elsewhere. Our data from Simcoe Bay have confirmed this. Respondents were asked to rate a number of job characteristics in terms of their importance when making a decision between two jobs which were offered to them. Their answers are presented together with the ratings of their own satisfaction with their current employment (Table 7.6). The job characteristics rated as most important, i.e., the security of job and pay, can potentially contribute more to overall satisfaction than others rated as not so important, such as the strength of the union, which is deemed to be of little consequence. 'Discrepancy scores' are presented in column (3) of Table 7.6. These scores were obtained by subtracting the importance score for each item from the corresponding satisfaction score. A higher rating indicates that the satisfaction score was greater than the importance score or, in other words, that a particular characteristic was not present in jobs to the degree that was desirable. A lower rating indicates that the discrepancy between the importance and satisfaction was less great, or that the desirable level had been achieved.

Table 7.6: Discrepancy Score between Satisfaction and Importance: JME (N=267)

	Satisfaction (1)	Importance (2)	Discrepancy (3) (1) - (2)
How you get on with management	2.7	1.9	0.8
The security of the job	3.0	1.3	1.7
How worthwhile the job is	2.7	1.7	1.0
How interesting the job is	2.7	1.5	1.2
Fringe benefits like pensions and sick pay	2.5	1.6	0.9
The friendliness of people you work with	2.1	1.6	0.5
Hours of work (including travel)	2.9	1.9	1.0
Your pay	3.2	1.5	1.7
Your working conditions	3.4	1.6	1.8
Training	3.5	2.0	1.5
Promotion chances	3.9	1.9	2.0
Trade union strength	3.4	2.8	0.6

While respondents at JME rated job security and pay among the most important job characteristics, discrepancy scores indicate that their concerns in these areas have not been met, or at least that these aspects of their employment are not viewed as satisfactory. They also assessed chances for promotion in their job as very important as well; yet such chances are unsatisfactory in their current employment. In the Canadian work values study (Burnstein, et al., 1975), the discrepancy score calculated through the factor analysis was highest in promotion opportunities, which is consistent with the present findings. Canadians were mostly dissatisfied and unhappy with the chances of promotion in their employment. The researchers (Burnstein, et al.:34) noted that, increasingly, a rigid system imposed by artificial hiring requirements, credentialism, and restrictive seniority rules limited the job mobility of many Canadians; employers were not seen to be fair and concerned about giving everyone a chance to get ahead.

Once workers accept that since they no longer can move to another firm, as is pretty well the case with employees at JME, the next logical step would seem to be to look for promotion within the company. However, expectations for getting ahead within the firm or without, for that matter, are not in fact in evidence. Employees' attitudes towards promotion at JME seem pretty similar to those described in the affluent worker study by Goldthorpe, et al. (1965). Workers in our study proved to be rather negative or pessimistic, and, for the large majority of those who were interviewed, promotion does not figure at all significantly in their future plans. Nothing resembling a success ladder seems to exist in factory work in general, explained some of the respondents, and JME is unlikely to promote them. One of the problems seems to be that JME's management has never clearly defined and presented a set of criteria for promotion within the company. Thus, few workers expect to be promoted. A female worker we interviewed with long years of service seems to have successfully adjusted her aspirations downward as she has come to grips with the fact that she will always remain a worker. She has found new interests in her life outside work, and ways of being happy in pursuing them.

> Probably you have to stay in the same firm to get anywhere. But here there's no chance really of getting anywhere. You can accumulate things like your holidays. It's just that you have to keep reminding yourself you do a factory job.

Many workers also accept that the bureaucratization of the enterprise and technical specialization make it impossible to achieve the goals of getting ahead.

> No way of getting ahead in a large workforce. You are actually a number. It doesn't matter who you are. It's just a waste of time, choosing anybody. They look for a supervisor and it seems to take them months to make a decision on whom they want. In a big place your chances of getting ahead are very small.

> In the same line of work I'd go anywhere in this plant. My age is against me in a lot of ways. I can't really do a heck of a lot in different places. So far as I am concerned, I'm stable here. If they want me to change from this job to another [in the work area] I'd go. There isn't another company like this around here, so I can't take skills and move them somewhere. I have my own side line at home.

> Not talking about changing jobs because I wouldn't know where else to go. I applied for a janitor's job but apparently they don't want the women doing janitors' work cause we couldn't lift heavy stuff. I liked the janitors' position because you weren't confined to one little room. You move around the plant which was good. If I tried to better myself, I would be afraid of worsening things.

Another indication of acceptance of the lack of opportunity for promotion was evident in the response to the question: "Five years from now, what would you like your job to be, if things went really well for you?" Seventy-seven per cent of the responding employees said that they would like their job to be in the same firm. This is consistent with the previous finding on the mobility prospect; the majority of workers viewed staying with the firm as the best policy to get ahead, whatever 'get ahead' may mean. Of those wishing to remain in the same firm, seventy-two per cent expected that they would be staying in the same line of work five years from now. About two-thirds of the remaining workers who would opt to be doing something different within the firm were divided into two groups in terms of their prospects. About two-thirds wanted to move to skilled or technicians' jobs as alternatives, and one-third wanted to be in supervisory positions. Thus, the highest level to which workers expect to be promoted with JME was either as a skilled trades man, some sort of specialist-technician, or as a supervisor, although the proportion of those expecting to achieve such positions was extremely small. Only seventeen individuals of all responding workers sought to become a supervisor. Not a single respondent elaborated on his/her expectation or desire of being promoted to supervisor in the course of the interview. At the operator's level the job most often cited as desirable was a janitor's job for the reasons provided in the quotation cited above. The idea of becoming a supervisor was not very appealing, as has been shown already in worker evaluation of supervisors in the previous chapter of this report. A number of workers at JME, like workers elsewhere (Goldthorpe, et al., 1965) felt that a promotion to a supervisory position could entail more trouble and responsibilities than it was worth. At the same time a few of the operators interviewed in this study have already been promoted to supervisory positions by the new management; so it seems that opportunities for advancement within the company are available, however small the chance may have seemed to employees.

The general lack of aspirations to promotions has struck and puzzled the Japanese management greatly. They see a sharp contrast in this respect between Japanese and Canadian workers. Workers with whom they are familiar in Japan, with the age-based seniority practice, look forward not only to higher wages as they get older but also toward promotion. Nearly all employees at JME in Japan aspire to higher positions, commented the president; while in Canada there appears to be less readiness and willingness to sacrifice personal life to higher ambitions. Cole (1971:103) noted that worker interest in being promoted to foreman amongst Japanese workers he studied becomes especially pronounced at age thirty-five. This gradual increase in the expectation of promotion with advancing age has profound consequences for increasing work satisfaction and providing effective incentives.

Of thirteen employment features measured in terms of work satisfaction, the figures in Table 7.1 indicate that workers at JME rated their chances of promotion the lowest. These workers were disillusioned and disappointed to find out that there was after all no standardized promotion system for them offered by the new management. With Arcan there never was a promotion system as such, but at least there were many more jobs from which workers could choose. Typically, following the American practice, Arcan management had created and worked with a job structure in which the skill differentials were minimized among operators' jobs. There existed about forty differentiated jobs; wages varied a mere few cents between jobs. Yet even with this minimized differential in skills and wages, employees had a sense that jobs were substantially different from each other. There were always some jobs more preferable than others in workers' views. Opportunities to move up from a lower job in the wage scale to a higher one, or to move to a more favourable job, were open to individuals.

JME reduced the number of jobs almost by half by creating fewer job classifications. Jobs under the Arcan structure looked just too numerous and cumbersome for Japanese management to handle. In the Japanese system job demarcations are much less rigidly defined, and jobs are categorized in a single-broad class covering a wide variety of tasks and responsibilities. Thus, creating seven instead of fourteen categories was a compromise worked out between the union and the company at the time JME signed the first labour contract. With no standardized promotion system and fewer jobs to move around, the president of the union commented that some workers felt extremely disappointed at the revised structure and even angry with management. According to the union president, knowing that one can transfer from one job to another every so often and feeling that a wide range of choices between jobs is available is very important for many workers, because liking or disliking a particular job varies greatly between individuals.

Our research has led us to believe that JME must create a reasonable structure based on wages and promotion in Simcoe Bay – a job grading system such as is widely used in Japan and transplanted into practice, for example, at Company A in Great Britain. This system is described by White and Trevor (1983:24):

> Production jobs up to charge-hand were divided into three broad grades, corresponding to skill or responsibility levels, and each of these in turn was subdivided into smaller steps, corresponding to levels of proficiency, so that there was a total of nine levels. Movement up this ranking depended on assessment by the individual's supervisor, and entitled the individual to a higher rate of pay.

According to the researchers, this method was in general favourably accepted by British workers.

How to promote personnel is closely related to how to train them. As we have discussed in earlier chapters, training is another area with which emloyees at JME show a considerable amount of dissatisfaction. British workers, on the other hand, were very impressed by the emphasis that their Japanese employer placed on training, and were extremely satisfied with the kind of training they received. In the British plant Japanese engineers and technicians were stationed to teach and consult with workers on the job. The training given in this way was said to be the most critical part of the entire training activities at the Japanese firm.

After surveying all of the Japanese-owned and managed auto assembling plants operating in the United States, Shimada and MacDuffie 1987) noted that selection and training of workers are "the questions of survival matter" for Japanese-managed plants, and thus have been emphasized greatly. The training typically provided to workers is an intensive and long-term process and involves several phases: preliminary vocational training, orientation sessions, introduction to Japanese mother plants, and on-the-job and off-the-job training.

Japanese firms overseas, like Company A in Great Britain, tend to build new plants of their own design and of a relatively small size, and seem to be able to promote young, inexperienced workers within a job grading system such as that as described above, keeping ambitious workers fairly satisfied. The kind of opportunities for promotion that tie in with learning experiences on the job increase work satisfaction among youthful employees. These are the kinds of results observed in the factories surveyed by Shimada and MacDuffie in the United States, and so far Japanese companies have created workable human resource management structures on their own and have enjoyed "peaceful and productive labor-management relations."

JME, which started with an established structure created by the former owner and employer, began with a relatively larger, more experienced work force. Instead of providing various forms of training such as documented by Shimada and MacDuffie in a systematic manner, the company largely relied on the work force with its ten-year record of service.

The Japanese management has admitted that the skills and experience of these workers have been "assets and beneficial to the operation" up to the present point, and particularly in the set-up period of the operation. However, in order to complete a major technical transfer process, with the constant movement toward modernization and computerization of the operation within the plant, management acknowledges that a new type of work force equipped with new skills and knowledge must emerge. With this in mind JME management both at head office in Japan and at the Simcoe Bay plant now recognize training as "the survival question." And this question is tied in with the problem of motivation of employees. Training and promotional opportunities must come before, or simultaneously with, the technical transfer process now being carried out. Creating a reasonable structure with new promotional opportunities tied to retraining seems one of the most urgent matters on the agenda for both management and the union in future contract negotiations.

Chapter Eight

The Simcoe Bay Plant as a Foreign-Owned Branch Plant

Arcan, the parent-founder of the Simcoe Bay plant, is a giant multinational enterprise with a number of divisions spread throughout the world. The Simcoe Bay plant was a part of the corporation's Electronic Components Division. It was also one of numerous branch plants, American-owned and controlled, operating in Canada. The Canadian electronics industry under investigation in this study had "a considerable and growing foreign ownership component" (Ontario Select Committee, 1973) in the early 1970s when the impact of foreign ownership on the industry was first thoroughly investigated by the government-commissioned study group,[1] and the overall picture has remained unchanged to the present. The consequences of foreign-controlled operations in Canada have been examined by governments as well as by scholars and students in the field, and have been an ongoing topic of debate. In the course of this scrutiny a few points have emerged as critical. They include: 1) the degree to which Canadian managerial skills remain undeveloped as a result of foreign control; 2) the degree of autonomy the Canadian subsidiaries are permitted to exercise; 3) the export and import performance of subsidiaries; 4) the effects of foreign subsidiaries upon Canadian research and development activities; and 5) the relative efficiency of foreign-controlled companies (English, 1971; Government of Canada, 1972; Ontario Select Committee,

1974). In this chapter we will attempt empirically to examine some of those points using the Simcoe Bay plant as a focal point of the examination and analysis, and more specifically, focusing on the issue of autonomy the plant was exercising under Arcan ownership and management. Through the discussion the legacy of American investment in this country will be probed. The major source of information for the discussion in this chapter is the material which was obtained from interviewing and informally talking with ex-managers of Arcan and with union executives.

A former senior manager with Arcan outlined the relationship between the Canadian subsidiary and its parent company:

> All the strategies and goals were set in X, the divisional headquarters. The production goal, in the case of Simcoe Bay making one million units for the year, for example, was set by the central office and communicated to us. The details of what Simcoe Bay would do exactly, and how we would do it, passed on to us through their internal communication network. We'd then sit down with the production goal in front of us to work out how x number of people in the organization would make x number of components a day at x amount of cost, the break-in points, and so on. We all knew what the other plants were doing and all tied in and all made sense. All of our reports went to the division.

This description indicates that the Simcoe Bay plant was not only directly and closely related to the parent company, but also highly dependent on the corporate strategy of the head office in the United States. According to this ex-manager, engineering and design standards, the quality and efficiency levels, the scrap level, and most other details were all dictated by head office personnel. They were the people who designed components and they were the people who worked with the customers. The procedures that the Canadian plant needed to know in order to follow the standards were passed on to the engineering personnel. The local personnel interfaced with Canadian customers who had different requirements from American customers through marketing personnel located in the Metropolitan area. Thus, a few standards were innovated by people specializing in standards located at the plant. But mostly those specialists were processing the papers coming from the States, with only a small amount of paper originated in Simcoe Bay. The use of imported designs was also noted in the Select

Committee study report as one of the significant differences in behaviour between the Canadian-and foreign-controlled companies it investigated (Select Committee, 1973: 76).

> The tendency of some foreign-controlled companies is to use basic designs developed by the parent and to concentrate research and development activity on devising means of efficiently scaling down production runs. This tendency is particularly prevalent in the consumer products area.

The electronics industry is international and the operation of the component segment is world wide. The ex-manager of Arcan described the marketing strategy and approach at Arcan as follows:

> Marketing data and other statistics which came through our Canadian customers were gathered and put together in Simcoe Bay. But, they tell you only a part of the whole story. All were sent up and fed into the central office. Marketing people in the central office were doing a world-wide business. They would look at the entire market and would tell us that we would have x number of units to make according to their forecasts.

Thus, all the relevant information locally gathered by the subsidiary was sent up to the divisional head office, where it was formulated into strategies for implementation, elaborated first into programs and then into activity plans. This indicates that the local plant played no role in determining either its overall market strategy even for the domestic market, or the methods to be used for achieving production targets. Local people had no part in policy-making; they were recruited to run the affairs of the branch plant by carrying out orders. Their role was described as that of "caretaker managers" by a worker on the shop floor. The caretaker manager had almost complete control over such areas as purchasing and choice of suppliers (however small the extent of the local supply itself might be), production planning, and labour negotiations in addition to the conduct of all aspects of day-to-day operations.

The process of decision-making involves various steps. In Paterson's (1966) framework of decision processes such steps as collecting information, processing information, making the choice, authorizing it, and executing it are outlined. Paterson argued that the power of those involved in the process is determined by the amount of control they have over these various steps. According to this framework, Arcan management in Simcoe Bay can be described as lacking control over the first four steps in decision-making. The amount of discretion available to the local plant seemed limited to the final step – implementing decisions made elsewhere. It seemed, in fact, so limited as to be almost negligible. So was the amount of power exercised.

Arcan founded the plant in Simcoe Bay to manufacture electronic components which were designed in the United States according to American specifications on production lines engineered by the American techno-structure. The products were standardized throughout the world, as were the engineering standards and procedures which were employed throughout the branch plants. The Simcoe Bay plant was, therefore, a replica – a carbon copy – of the company's other component manufacturing plants operating in various national markets. It was duplicated in Canada primarily to serve the national market ('getting behind' the Canadian tariff), and specialized in a few types of products, but on a smaller scale than its American counterparts. Arcan plants everywhere were nonetheless performing the same activities in the same ways.

The plant manager as well as senior staff managers met with their American counterparts regularly, according to the respondent, and at these meetings they could offer suggestions and make proposals for projects. At Arcan, however, all major projects had to receive an individual appropriation from the head office. Final decisions were based on overall corporate performance and were made by the corporate executives. A trend in large multinational companies, particularly those with head offices in the United States, was to move toward more and more integration of the entire world-wide operation (Ontario Select Committee). The Canadian subsidiary was becoming increasingly subject to the close scrutiny of the parent organization, which led to a trend toward a reduction in the autonomy of subsidiaries.

The decision to close the Simcoe Bay plant was "one of those corporate decisions" made by the headquarters of the multinational in New York.

> The decision was made at the U.S. headquarters. Nobody, including the Canadian president, was actually involved in the process of decision-making. Nobody locally had any say whatsoever. Here at the Simcoe Bay plant everybody was involved in the operations, not in the real decision-making. We were doing what we were told to do.

That the decision was highly and almost exclusively political was a view shared by practically everybody involved in the plant operation. Political pressure was brought to bear in the United States in the midst of the recession with the declining demand in the world wide market. "The U.S. government wanted to keep the jobs in the United States; so they pressured Arcan to consolidate their manufacturing activities." Though not an official version, one version of the story which was widely circulated and believed in the community, according to a veteran worker, was that the company first decided to close one of their American plants. But the U.S. government said "No": "This is an American company. You have to keep American people working in it. Close your foreign plants down. So we were the ones that died first." In this way nearly 900 jobs were lost through the closure, and they were transferred to the home country of the multinational.

It was unanimously accepted among the local personnel in Simcoe Bay that the Canadian plant was not closed because it was not making a profit. Ex-Arcan employees faced with the announcement of the closure had confidence that the plant was profitable, which was later proved by a study conducted by a consulting firm. Although the result of the study was considered confidential and thus never revealed to the public, the study reached the conclusion that Arcan's Canadian operation was profitable, and that any firm taking over the operation could likely be highly profitable. Thus, the argument went that the business or economic considerations had very little to do with the decision to close the plant. Because it was highly political and not based on business considerations, the decision turned out to be very "poor" and proved to be very "short-sighted." For it was not very long after the closure of the plant that the market turned around. The reasons people gave for believing that the decision to shut down was political, not economic, are strikingly similar to the one that was elaborated by Grayson (1985) in his case study of the plant closure. The point to be emphasized here nonetheless is that local personnel were not in a position to give adequate consideration to the business or economic side of such a multinational operation, and they had no say whatsoever on the future state of the enterprise, nor control over their own fate.

A subsidiary established by multinational corporations seldom performs all the critical functions which a major corporation requires for its operation (Government of Canada, 1972:42-43). In the case of the Arcan plant, as indicated in the former manager's statement cited above, the plant was not responsible for product development or marketing. New equipment and new production processes developed by headquarter engineers were first installed in home plants. Subsequent installation of new equipment and new processes in other plants was phased in with the firm's most important plants receiving the capital required first. Since the Simcoe Bay plant was a "peaking plant," serving Canada and the offshore markets when it was sensible to do so, it was likely that technology changed even less frequently at Simcoe Bay than at other Arcan plants. As a result, the subsidiary was limited in scope and potential, yet production based on imported designs may have resulted in better and less expensive products. Thus, this was viewed "as one of the advantages" by at least one of the senior managers with Arcan:

> They [the head office] tried out new things, i.e., new designs, in the States first. If it looked good, then it would come up from another plant to us. They helped us put it up. That was one of the advantages we had. We were the last one to get anything new, so we didn't make the same mistakes. We always did a good job of introducing new technology, better than the American plants.

Product development and marketing were vital to the existence of the Canadian subsidiary, but activities were centralized in and retained by the divisional office in the United States. Because of the pattern established in the past, no room was perceived for creating and developing necessary research-related services in the Canadian operation, at least in local personnel's minds. The Simcoe Bay plant was really a branch plant in that it was largely a "truncated" enterprise, or a "headless subsidiary – one with no control over its main strategies" (Mintzberg, 1979:397). This left the subsidiary plant "fewer export opportunities, fewer supporting services, less training of local personnel in various skills, less specialized product development aimed at Canadian needs or tastes and less spillover economic activity" (Government of Canada, 1971: 42-43).

Within the parameters established by head office, the Canadian managers at Arcan felt that they had considerable freedom of action to run their own affairs, but only as long as they availed themselves of the authorization, assistance and protection provided by the parent company for the operation. At Simcoe Bay, as one of the workers on the shop floor observed, the parent company's direct input seemed indispensible in the critical areas associated with the technical side of production:

> When they had any serious problems, quality or engineering problems, they conferred with the States. They could always pick up the phone and call the central office for help. People were able to get assistance. That was the way they solved their problem.

Dependent organizations, i.e., foreign-owned subsidiaries, tend to have a more centralized authority structure and tend to be more bureaucratic (Mintzberg, 1979). This is because control of the corporate head office tends to concentrate decision-making power at the top of the organizational hierarchy and to encourage greater than usual reliance on rules and regulations for internal control. An example was provided by another ex-Arcan manager:

> For the management training program I participated in, packaged course materials used as a text book, prepared by the head office, were used throughout the branches. Arcan's policy was to get all the branches reading and singing out of the same hymn book. It is getting everybody doing the same sort of thing. In doing that you can have a strong team.

At the Canadian plant there were many different kinds of operating manuals; most were used globally, but some only in the plant, and they were issued to all employees to whom they would be relevant, giving standard methods and operating procedures. Head office insisted on these standards being applied across the whole range of organizations it controlled. A common organization chart (as presented in Chapter Three of this report), and a common management information system were adopted by the branch organizations. Management training and personnel development programs were "corporate programs" created by the head office. A set of purchasing regulations, job descriptions and reporting relationships were specified and passed down to the branch plant. A host of programs, such as worker training, employee suggestions, and the quality-circle (two-way meetings), just to name a few identified by the informants, were initiated by industrial relations personnel in the central office and implemented by the branch. These tangible standards and programs imposed on the branch plant, in turn, bureaucratized the structure of the organization.

A foreign-owned enterprise acts differently from a solely Canadian-owned company for various reasons (Government of Canada, 1972; Government of Ontario, 1973; Watkins, 1968; Safarian, 1966). One reason could be the differences in the organizational structure under which each operates, a dimension which has received little attention in previous studies in this country. How different is the structure that management of parent corporations introduce in their subsidiaries from that of national corporations in terms of major design features? Are the coordinating mechanisms significantly different between, for instance, American-and Japanese-owned branch plants? The answers to these questions can only be obtained from empirical and systematic investigation by examining a number of comparable organizations. Although it deals with only one case, what the present study has demonstrated is that the differences in design adopted by the two foreign-owned organizations are substantial and significant (Chapter 3). Under the new management at JME strategic planning is now done within the Canadian plant, not at the company headquarters, and marketing as well is done in Simcoe Bay. How successful the new company will be in pursuing these critical activities remains largely to be seen in the years to come. Behavioural patterns at JME differing significantly from the ones at Arcan may indeed emerge in due course.

Standardization of work processes and output, the means used at Arcan to achieve coordination, substantially limited the discretion available to the management of the Canadian branch organization. This form of coordination assigned to the managers in charge the role of assuring that the standardized procedures were implemented. They were not allowed to act as innovators. The component manufacturing industry that these people were involved in, however, depends on a high level of technological innovation for success. The employees of the American-controlled organization developed neither the skills and capacities of potential innovators, nor a management orientation which stressed innovation, because the plant did not seek to perform such critical tasks as product development and research. In large part the organization operated as though it were a closed system with few linkages to customers, suppliers and markets.

The plant manager with JME commented on the consequences of standardizing work in the Arcan manner:

> Arcan never developed, even with all those people, the deep, technical personnel in this factory. If they got a problem, they phoned the States, the outside help to solve it. The man was here the next day, and some specialist sorted out the problem for them, telling them to 'do like that.' No one really acquired fully complete technical expertise that way. We hoped at the outset that we would have resources in house here, to solve some of the problems, but it doesn't seem so. The basic theoretical understanding of the component design was not really here.

A young engineer newly employed by JME witnessed the same thing. The behaviour pattern as he sees it has been causing some problems:

> The ex-Arcan people hired back [by JME] are not designers. I guess they never had any experience in designing. They had never needed it. Arcan engineering was somewhere else where designing was done. Whenever there was a problem, these guys would come zooming out and fix it and go back to the States.

The plant was, in fact, "too well" controlled from the United States. Local management had not acquired sufficient skills and capacities to "stand on their own feet technically," nor to support even their own enterprise when they were left alone. Was Arcan then an extreme case of foreign-controlled subsidiaries operating in Canada? The question was raised by one of the Japanese expatriate engineers. He explains what he feels are the inadequacies of the ex-Arcan managers and engineers:

> The managerial orientation acquired during the Arcan years seems to dictate the behaviour patterns of the managers. I

suspect that they were only following the instructions and orders coming from X. 'Wait and see what X says.' Was that their way of thinking and doing the jobs here? Perhaps locals never needed to take the initiative. 'The frog in the well does not know the ocean.' Their minds had been blocked or closed against seeing the outside world of their market, customers, new design developments, etc. I suspect that the technological innovation or development of new products by local initiatives was done very little in this plant.

The poor performance in research and development activities in this country has been noted as one of the effects of the presence of subsidiaries of foreign corporations (Bourgault, 1972) because those activities tend to be carried out by the parent company at its home offices. Research and development programs pursued at the subsidiary are often aimed at adapting the products developed by the parent for a more limited scale of production in Canada. In these circumstances, the research and development effort rarely leads to innovative outputs of a type which would make their products competitive in the world market. A circular effect seems to be at work here: because this has historically been the pattern in the past, the necessary research-related activities and services have not been adequately developed in Canada; the lack of development, in turn, has caused additional research to be carried out in the home country of the parent company. It is, in fact, cheaper and more economical for the subsidiary to utilize the innovations developed by the parent company than to develop its own.

Physically isolated, although not too far from the nation's largest metropolis, Simcoe Bay is not an area where first-class engineers would be attracted to come and make a career. A young engineer noticed it immediately upon arriving at the area: "In this area, not only in this factory alone, there are no real engineers." The closest technical school is thirty miles away, and the closest university is in Metropolis. "There is no real technological updating you can do in this area, other than a few long distance phone calls." This young technician admitted that he does not even feel like telephoning, because it is a too costly investment both in time and expense. This may make him "a frog in the well that does not know the ocean," as the Japanese engineer depicted, and the technician's mind may become blocked or closed against seeing the outside world.

When Arcan built the Simcoe Bay plant in 1966, it was the world's most advanced plant. Back in Japan in 1960, according to a company document, JME's first color television was produced at one of its plants, incorporating technologies developed by Arcan. To the great surprise and disappointment of the Japanese engineers in probing the 20-year operation of the Canadian plant since its opening, however, the basis of product design had remained unchanged, and "no signs of cumulative innovations" were found.

> We came to this plant with the expectation of learning something new, something unique to Arcan, the world leader of component manufacturing. Sorry to say, but no signs of accumulative innovations and of design change have been found. They had only a few standard kinds of components to make, and the same process was done over and over again. The confidence acquired at the time when this plant was built, appeared to be sustained without having pressure from the outside.

The expatriate engineer's remarks suggest that Arcan had not had major and capital investment after its production facilities were well established in the early stage. Some other engineers described the Simcoe Bay plant as "a 1966 Ford." In assessing the case of a bearing-manufacturing plant which was owned and closed by a multinational company, Grayson (1985) maintained that this lack of investment was obvious in that company as well. And that was one of the signs, argued Grayson, that the multinational would close the Canadian plant, and one of the reasons the operation was less profitable than it could have been. Likewise, Arcan was forced to close its subsidiary plant, according to some employees, because it had failed to achieve the level of competitiveness, technical as well as non-technical, to remain in business. What is thus becoming evident is that the decision to close the Simcoe Bay plant may have had more to do with business reasons than has previously been understood.

The Japanese engineer's remarks quoted above also stress the consequences of the legacy of American investment and American organizational design. It created Canadian managers and technicians in particular, who "do not get pressure from the outside and do not see the outside world," and thus are insensitive to the need for change and lack the skills and experience required to redesign the product and marketing. Whatever change occurred was fragmented and not ongoing. And it was not initiated by the employees in Simcoe Bay. Whenever change occurred, it was imposed from headquarters and designed by a foreign techno-structure with little or no input from local employees. Without an adequate re-tooling and updating with the current level of technology, no business enterprise can survive in the type of industry under investigation.

JME's Simcoe Bay plant is expected, as the plant manager sees it, to "stand on [its] own feet technically" and to "do a lot of [its] own market research and design development so [it] can go after the North American business." The company also tries to establish "close and lasting" business relationships with local suppliers. Up to this point JME has been importing most parts from their factories in Japan, a tendency which is more prevalent in foreign- than Canadian-controlled companies (Ontario Select Committee; 1973). This is due, in part, to the use of imported designs in foreign-controlled companies. The JME management would like to build up an exclusive relationship with local long-run suppliers. Management has come to realize that a supplier base in the locality of Simcoe Bay is almost non-existent, and that the company has to go out of its way to look for possible suppliers. The search alone has taken more time than the company had expected at the outset, and to build up lasting business relationships and "work together with them for product development" will require still more time. JME's office in Japan continues to function as a production consultant, but in due course it will increasingly delegate responsibilities to the Canadian locality as it gets firmly established technically. "We are expected to devise our own ways of increasing efficiency, and develop forms of production here locally." This exists because of the physical distance between the two operations, and also, partly at least, because the head office in Japan knows very little about the North American market. The Simcoe Bay plant is thus viewed as a reservoir of expertise. Selective decentralization is deemed appropriate so that such expertise can be utilized effectively. The Japanese corporate culture prescribes a longer-term commitment to the local as well as the national community: "We have come here and will be here for a long, long time." Such a view promotes development of long-term linkages with domestic suppliers as well as customers.

Note

1. In the Select Committee report (1973; 33) the Canadian electronics industry in the early 1970s with regard to foreign-ownership was described as follows: Canada was competitive internationally in a fairly narrow range of electronics products. Foreign-owned companies accounted for less than half of the total output of the industry as a whole. This was well below that in many other high-technology industries in Canada. Nonetheless foreign-owned firms in the industry tended to be larger and more profitable than Canadian-controlled companies on the average. Of the twenty or so largest companies in the industry, which together accounted for approximately three quarters of the total output, only four were Canadian-controlled. The industry is very scale dependent. The larger the output of an operation, the more profitable it becomes. As a result of this, larger foreign-owned firms tended to be more profitable than Canadian-controlled firms. The scale-dependent consumer electronics industry has been hampered by the presence of foreign-controlled firms in particular, because they contributed to a severe fragmentation of the industry.

Chapter Nine
Summary of Findings and Implications

JME, the Japanese firm under investigation, chose (or was forced to choose) a constrained approach to the introduction of Japanese management. This is in contrast to other Japanese companies, which almost always choose to adopt an unconstrained approach to the introduction of Japanese management by building their own overseas plants from scratch. JME purchased a factory and machinery designed by the former owner rather than by itself. It accepted a Canadian government loan and grant and, in return, agreed to keep the regular work force intact and to recognize the existing union and the overall institutional framework of labour-management relations which had been previously established. The company further agreed to recall workers on the basis of seniority, and started the operation with a work force largely consisting of those recalled workers. As a result of these constraints, the Canadian subsidiary has been unable to transfer to its new plant the production processes and management system of its parent plant at the pace and to the degree that the management had anticipated. Rather, the Japanese-owned plant has been faced with the need to redesign both the production process and the management system to accommodate the constraints.[1]

Obviously this adoption of a constrained approach has had some advantages – for example, purchasing an existing facility with a work force already in place considerably reduced the lead time required to open a manuacturing facility. At the same time, however, the unforseen problems arising from this situation have been numerous, and should be very instructive to other firms thinking of taking the same approach.

To begin with, the need to redesign existing facilities and machinery has proven to be a difficult and costly task. It has required much more sensitivity to the differences between the Japanese and Canadian environments than would have been required by the mere replication of Japanese production processes and management systems developed by the head office. Integrating American and Japanese equipment in the early stages of operation, adopting a trial-and-error process with one set of equipment after another, and interfacing between machines and workers have also taken much longer and required more effort than the new management had estimated. Also, the American-sized plant overwhelmed Japanese engineers at the beginning and it was not easy for them to overcome the inconvenience, "There are a lot of conveyors to connect and they are too far apart to use robotics and transfer devices." The problems in formulating the configurations of machines, new and old, small and large, have been many.

Despite the substantial constraints under which it has had to work, and despite its difficulties in implementing a Japanese technology and management system, JME has nevertheless had some substantial successes in its five years of operation. In particular, the changes introduced by Japanese management to increase the amount of production of the Simcoe Bay plant and to become profitable have been quite fruitful (Chapter Three). In the summer of 1987, three-and-a-half years after the beginning of production, the plant was producing approximately four thousand units a day, the highest level ever achieved, surpassing by about five hundred units the record attained by the former company. To attain this level of production output was given high priority by the company for the initial stage. With the continuous introduction of new automated equipment and other labour-saving techniques, the company has recently claimed to be nearing the level of production and productivity of its home plant. The production capacity of the plant for its size being about "1.5 to 2 million components a year," this may well be a reality by 1990. This rapidly increasing productivity is a major accomplishment for the fledgling Canadian subsidiary, something for which it can be congratulated.

The company has met and even exceeded its production targets while operating with considerably reduced staffing levels, levels which were set by the head office in Tokyo. Thus, the improvement in production has been matched by a considerable improvement in productivity; the organization has been restructured to drastically reduce the size of the work force on the shop floor as well as the administrative staff. The company has managed to introduce the "leanest possible structure" to its Simcoe Bay plant, bringing it closer to the Japanese model. This has been a major factor in raising productivity to a level which is considered competitive relative to other component producers in the world market.

It should be noted, however, that improved productivity so far has occurred at JME primarily as a result of a tremendous upgrading of machines and equipment. The prime mandate of the Canadian management was to modernize the "1966 Ford" type of factory which it inherited. Under the management of the former company the basics of hardware remained unchanged within the plant for the twenty years of its operation, and there was very little upgrading of technology. The gap between the worldwide trend of the industry toward factory automation and what was actually observed at the Simcoe Bay plant was obvious and indeed grave. To narrow the gap, JME has emphasized increasing automation and modernization, something which has been made possible by the continued reinvestment committed and endorsed by the company's head office. Therefore, direct and exact transfer in the area of hardware has been done as much as possible.

Considerably less emphasis, on the other hand, has been placed on improving the interaction between technology and human resources. We have witnessed and documented this in the process of detailing the changes made by the new company and assessing their consequences. No doubt there was (and still is) genuine interest on the part of the company to find ways in which to improve their own approaches to human resources in the future, if not immediately. However, the extent of that development has so far been extremely limited. At the outset management had assumed employees would accept change more readily if it was undertaken gradually, step by step, rather than rapidly. However, phasing in changes has meant that changes have occurred in a piecemeal rather than a comprehensive, integrated fashion. This has made it more difficult for employees to understand the new directions in which the plant is headed and the reasons for the package of changes being introduced. The piecemeal approach to changing the systems of job classification, job rotation and seniority (Chapter Four), for example, has had less than satisfactory results. We could go as far as to say that it has had a number of troubling consequences and has led to a fair amount of strain for all those involved in this process of transition.

First of all, the piecemeal introduction and implementation of changes has reduced the degree of consistency among design parameters of the organization. This inconsistency, together with the ad hoc approach to dealing with the overall change, has impeded in a fundamental way the transition in the structure of the organization from a bureaucratic to a flexible structure, or to put it differently, to a structure closer to the "Japanese model" with which the top management would be most familiar and comfortable. The new ways of doing things JME has introduced or attempted to introduce, such as the QC method and job rotation, could only be fully effective if a flexible structure were employed by them. For various reasons, however, fundamental changes in the human resources area have not occurred within the organization. Thus, for example, management still painstakingly complies with the seniority rule in assigning jobs and promotion instead of estblishing a new job structure. And yet it seems clear that to achieve effective production Japanese-style working practices and Japanese-style management, together with hardware technology, must be "part and parcel of one concerted system" (White and Trevor, 1983: 132). "If human resources fail to play effective roles in the system," the entire system, predicted Shimada and MacDuffie (1987:6), "will not operate properly and will lose its efficiency." This has been well proven to be the case at Simcoe Bay.

The decision to address the technological issues before the human resource issues at the Simcoe Bay plant has resulted in reducing employee understanding of how Japanese and American management assumptions in manufacturing differ from one another. At various points of discussion throughout this report the differences in assumptions have been brought up and articulated in an attempt to lead to some insight into the nature of the discordance between Japanese and American management. Our conclusion is simple: better understanding of the differences in assumptions between the two systems is the key to a smooth and effective transition from one to the other.

The differences appear to be the most substantial and critical in the area of the practice of quality and productivity control. The former American management, represented by Arcan, sought to improve the production processes by improving the understanding of what can go wrong, of sources of error. To control error, there was an emphasis on monitoring people and machinery so that error could be detected early and corrected rapidly. In that way resources would not be wasted. The American management measured quantity of error-free output (output scrap) and thus used this as their major performance standard. Scrap represented failure and was analyzed. The responsibility for error could be assigned and controls needed to reduce error could be imposed.

The new Japanese management, on the other hand, is seeking to improve the production process by meshing people and machines so that their activities complement one another. The object is to improve continually the links between one process and another. Automation is valued because it facilitates consistent quality. Managers and supervisors manage and supervise processes rather than people. They seek to reallocate people so that processes can be integrated more effectively. Neither machinery nor people are underutilized. Japanese management measures the ratio of output with which customers are satisfied to the number of employees. Quality results when customer needs are understood and met, and when the production processes for meeting these needs are effectively coordinated. Their emphasis is thus not on errors and their detection.

In the American system of management, new technologies are developed by engineers and specialists (thinkers) segregated from production personnel (doers), and introduced at discrete intervals. Under Arcan, the two groups of personnel engaged in production activities were kept apart physically and otherwise and thus there was a distinct division of labour between them. Under this system, when new technologies are introduced, old plants become obsolete. In these circumstances the likelihood is that the plant will close or threaten to close, as Arcan did, in order to get government grants and worker concessions to reduce the cost of re-tooling and upgrading for modernization.

Japanese management assumes the continuous upgrading of technology by encouraging all employees constantly to search for better ways of doing things. According to this view a plant does not become obsolete, because through feedback and mutual adjustment technology, organization and production processes as a unit change continuously and together. Thus, specifications are also perpetually changing in response to the implementation of proposals for improvement. In this way quality and productivity are improved through an ongoing redesign in which workers and management participate in jointly making and refining proposals.

American management assumes that engineers are the ones to establish specifications to program worker behaviour. These specifications change infrequently, particularly at a branch plant. Quality control personnel and supervisors monitor worker behaviour and engage in error detection and error control to ensure that workers and machines comply with specifications. The major role of supervisors is to give instructions and orders (a one-way communication), to coordinate through direct supervision, and to motivate workers.

Under Japanese management, supervisors have a very different role. Instead of engaging in error detection and control, the supervisors' role is to liaise with others (Chapter Five). Since workers are supposed to be experts and to both think and do, they require more information. A supervisor gathers and shares information, so that work groups can quickly adjust to one another. Supervisors and workers coordinate through two-way meetings, i.e., through daily shift meetings on the shop floor. Worker motivation is not a supervisor's job, because workers are assumed to be well motivated. Their motivation derives from the opportunity afforded them by management to contribute to making things better and from their perception that their job is a career providing increasingly worthy work. This motivation is said to come from new training, jobs, rewards, and from the active participation in the process of organizing the work.

The above constitute the major differences in assumptions which have emerged in the course of data analyses and discussion in this study. Our data on the practice of quality control most clearly indicate that Canadian workers and supervisors alike at JME under Japanese management lack an understanding of the differences in assumptions underlining the American and Japanese approaches to production work. This lack of understanding has had some important implications for the behaviour of both workers and supervisors. These workers, most of whom are familiar with the American method, need to understand why there are no specifications or training of the kind provided by the American management, why the Japanese try to get things going rather than fixing them, and why cooperation and teamwork are so essential to the success of the Japanese system. If these differences were explained and communicated, the workers would be in a better position to understand, if not accept, the Japanese approach to achieving quality and to realize that quality will improve when they focus on improving the process and the flows rather than on monitoring faults and on diagnosing the cause of these faults.

The reasons for this deep-seated misunderstanding of the system JME has attempted to introduce are complex but understandable. Since most of the workers hired by JME were former Arcan employees, they had to begin by "unlearning" some deeply rooted aspects of American management methods in order to accept the system being introduced by Japanese management. This process was difficult for various reasons. The literature indicates that there are multiple ways in which members of an organization are socialized or resocialized. Ex-Arcan managers, supervisors, and workers alike were expected under Japanese production management to learn a way of doing things and the rational for this way of doing things which was very new and different from that with which they were familiar under American management. They were expected to acquire role behaviours appropriate to newly defined job assignments and responsibilities. Yet these expectations were never clearly stated. Indeed nobody really seems to have understood the necessity for resocialization of the employees at Simcoe Bay. Who after all was in charge of the business of resocialization?

The top management deemed resocialization to be an employee rather than an employer responsibility. It assumed that employees with years of service and experience in the field already knew how they were expected to behave in the company, and that they required no reorientation. Thus, only inadequate attention has been devoted to defining the differences in assumptions between the new and old systems. Likewise, the employees seem not to have been aware of the acute need for resocialization. After all, they returned to the plant with "the same walls and the same machinery," and with very few visible changes. They expected, rightly or wrongly, to encounter much greater visible change than they found. With fewer dramatic technological and organizational changes than expected, with the possible exception of the reduced work force, change was categorized as being quantitative rather than qualitative, a change in emphasis or priorities rather than a fundamentally different way of doing and viewing things. And because Japanese management has built upon American management principles and North American practices of industrial relations, it did not seem that alien to the workers. It was easy then to argue that all that had changed was the definition of acceptable trade-offs. In the eyes of most workers, therefore, the two employers differed in the weight each assigned to such factors as working practices and procedures. Under these circumstances JME's practices seemed only slightly different from those of the previous management. The nature and magnitude of the differences were underestimated. Thus, no provisions existed for resocialization to take place.

The result of this lack of communication was perhaps predictable. As the magnitude of the changes JME wanted to make began to sink in, employees reacted by passive, and sometimes even active, resistance. In organizational change the most difficult part is implementation (Daft, 1983). We discovered in the course of our research that many aspects of Japanese human resource management which JME planned to introduce were simply never implemented. To begin with, top management appears not to have completely worked out the specific changes that they intended to introduce and they certainly had not anticipated nor developed strategies to deal with resistance to change by local personnel. Our impression was that no special plans or provisions were being made by the company to get their working practices accepted in their labour agreement with the union either. White and Trevor (130) also noted the seeming lack of preparation for anticipated problems by Japanese companies that they studied in Great Britain.

In times of change, resistance is often encountered in any organization, and the Simcoe Bay plant was no exception. This resistance was perhaps most obvious in the area of supervision by supervisors on the production line (Chapter Five). Supervisors had difficulty both adjusting to the increased responsibilities imposed upon them by the new management and coping with the role conflict and ambiguity which they normally experience. These problems were derived in large part from the differences in the way that the work is organized under the two management systems.

Under the Japanese system production processes are changing rather than fixed, adjusting to conditions surrounding the plant operation. These changes constantly give rise to fresh problems and unforeseen requirements for action; so rules must be flexible. Action plans and rules cannot simply be written down and distributed automatically. The supervisor's role in handling these changes must be to implement the change at the task level and ensure that new machinery and tools operate correctly, that workers understand the new process and that quality standards are maintained under the new technology. Therefore, under the new management, both the responsibilities and the discretion of the supervisors were substantially increased. This was not necessarily perceived as desirable by the JME supervisors, however. Some refused to accept the new ways and the roles newly expected of them. This resistance was shown either in a passive way through a general indifference to the new ideas so that nothing was ever done about them, or by an active denial of the value of the new system, both in its physical design and in its management of human resources.

Workers on the shop floor also showed a fair amount of resistance to change, though for different reasons than those given by supervisors. Perhaps because of JME's failure to explain its new policies, most workers seem to prefer the Arcan approach to work practices, and are extremely reluctant to discard the old ways of doing things for the new. This reaction to change seems to be due as much to their overall dissatisfaction with their employment (Chapter Seven) as to their resistance to the new management. Naturally this dissatisfaction or discontent was most evident among the ex-Arcan employees at Simcoe Bay. Our study has uncovered that Canadian workers under JME's Japanese management, unlike their British counterparts, are, in general unhappy, and dissatisfied with their employment: JME employees rated themselves considerably less satisfied than did the British workers. Worker dissatisfaction was particularly directed toward job security, pay and working conditions. The contrast between the Canadian and British workers under Japanese management was most marked in this regard.

JME employees were disillusioned and disappointed at the revised job structure created by the new management. While it eliminated many positions at the high end of the pay scale, including most of the Quality Control personnel and some relief positions, and thus greatly reduced the work force overall, management did not compensate for this perceived limitation in the possibility of job advancement for workers on the shop floor by creating any kind of new promotion system. This has left the workers, the large majority of whom are strongly attached to their present employment, with a job structure that does not provide them with anything close to a career. JME has still not introduced any long-term policies on career structures and career development. While jobs at JME are regarded as exceptionally secure by local standards because of the company's no lay-off policy, workers are not impressed; they show no sense of security and appreciation. As with their former employer, the workers still have jobs rather than careers. JME would be well-advised to reassess its job structure to provide a system of incentives and compensation that would give workers a sense of the possibility of advancement. Providing a career is different from creating job security. The change from a mere job holder to a career pursuer involves fundamental conceptual changes in assessing what work means to each individual. A well-developed career structure would entice some ambitious workers not only to stay longer in the organization, but to get involved in the operational process by willingly providing their input. These individuals would then become indispensible to the organization through their contribution to the development and refinement of production processes. Needless to say, this is still not the case at JME.

The result is that JME is faced with a disappointed and frustrated work force. The problem is largely one of its own making, derived from "a half-hearted application of Japanese management methods" because, as White and Trevor's study (133) indicates, workers employed by Japanese companies in fact want more, not less, of the Japanese approach. Canadian and British workers do not differ in this regard. At Simcoe Bay the workers want to see a whole-hearted approach in dealing with the reorganization of the plant structure.

Participation in organizational change gives those involved a sense of control over the change activity. They understand it better, and they become committed to its successful implementation. To increase the chance of successful implementation, early and extensive participation in the change should be part of the implementation strategy. At JME participation should have begun in the initial stages before production started, so that ideas, assumptions and proposals from Japanese management could be presented to and debated with employees, and those from employees could be incorporated in the management's design changes. Management could have implemented some major aspects of production management and work practices in a shorter period with more efficiency by letting employees be more heavily involved in the implementation process from the very beginning.

Successful implementation of change also requires open channels of communication. Management should have explained what steps would be taken to ensure that the changes would have no adverse consequences for employees. They should have provided far more information than they did about the consequences of the proposed changes and about any foreseeable "problems" to be encountered in due course. Full disclosure and detailed explanations might have prevented the false rumours, misunderstandings and resentment which we were privy to during the course of our research. This system of open channels of communication could have been established through the daily shift meetings between workers and supervisors and monthly meetings between employees and management which JME introduced. However, since JME failed even to explain the purpose of these meetings adequately to its employees, this opportunity was lost, and both workers and supervisors now express dissatisfaction with these meetings.

The point of the argument stated above does not mean to insist that there is an optimal way for the JME plant to operate, that is, just like the Japanese do at their home plant in Japan, or that if all Japanese methods and practices had been consistently incorporated into the operations, the plant would be more likely to be problem-free. The top management of JME would not act based on such assumptions either. It would be too simplistic to assume that the "Japanese model" as such, even in its totality, would effect the same outcome as in Japan. The "Japanese way" seems to be, nonetheless, the only way for the top management as they "would not know otherwise."

The insights and implications of this case study are, we believe, extremely valuable both for Japanese firms seeking a foothold in North America and for their potential Canadian partners, including employees, trade unions, various levels of government, and suppliers of both services and materials.

There are several important implications for Japanese firms, first of all. Perhaps the most obvious is that they must be prepared to expend a lot more time and energy than they have estimated in the past to set up a plant in Canada, and to introduce and implement their distinctive management practices. In the case presently being studied, the number of constraints which JME experienced has meant that the amount and quality of management effort required to implement its management style and methods while integrating Japanese and American production systems has been a much more demanding task than the company ever anticipated. The constraints encountered by JME have made it exceedingly difficult for the firm to design an organization which best fits its needs, both in terms of physical set-up and human resources.

The problems encountered by JME in taking over an existing North American plant are, in short, staggering, and would seem to discourage other Japanese firms from following their example. At first glance the lesson learned by JME, to be taken to heart by other firms thinking of establishing branch plants in North America, seems to be that it is better to set up a plant from scratch – to come to a "greenfield," where they will encounter no constraints to the introduction of their management and methods, and to hire workers with no previous experience in the concerned industry. In fact, the difficulty associated with the redesigning of production facilities alone is said to be the major reason why Japanese manufacturers operating overseas are deterred from taking over existing plants. These difficulties encourage them to build, instead, their own manufacturing facilities from their own designs, and to replicate almost exactly the hardware technology and production systems of their home country.

However, the problems encountered by JME in taking over an existing plant were far from insurmountable. With a little foresight and preparation, the company could have avoided many of the problems which have plagued it over the last five years. These problems began with its piecemeal introduction of intended changes. JME had no management techniques in place for introducing the proposed changes to its Canadian subsidiary and employees and for implementing these changes from the outset. It did not invest sufficient time or human resources to developing a viable and understandable proposal for change, and in so doing committed a serious error in judgment.

The critical factor missing at JME in its efforts to introduce its technology and to integrate this technology with the existing American-designed system appears to have been a direct and intensive interaction between Japanese expertise and local employees. JME should have sent more technicians and engineers from the home plant to the Simcoe Bay plant, and for a longer period, in order to facilitate the process of transformation and to train the local staff. These engineers could have provided on-the-job reorientation sessions that would have introduced and explained the differences in product methods and assumptions to the workers. One of the findings of the British study is that the success with which Japanese practices and management style are introduced is directly related to the number of Japanese expatriates working at each site, and to the number of local employees trained by these expatriates.

The head office of JME in Tokyo endorses a policy of what they call 'localization,' directing its subsidiaries operating overseas to employ local personnel and to adopt local employment practices as much as possible. Thus, it regards the need for Japanese expatriates at its Canadian plant as, at best, temporary. In its view, a successful reorganization entails that the positions temporarily filled by the Japanese will be permanently filled by local employees. The sooner this replacement takes place, the better the operation becomes in the view of the head office.

Having entered the fifth year in its operation, however, localization at Simcoe Bay still seems to be far from completely being attained. The Canadian company must have a supply of trained, qualified personnel on hand. Without an abundant supply of human expertise, it will have a hard time producing output. And yet managerial talent as well as engineering expertise have constantly been in short supply in the small isolated community of Simcoe Bay. The need for continuous training and guiding of Canadian employees, of managers and supervisors in particular, has increased rather than decreased in the five years the plant has been operating. The need for training engineers newly hired by JME and retraining the ex-Arcan engineers seems critical for building up "a solid engineering base" within the plant, especially since the plant is expected to be responsible for its own product development to go after a North American market. White and Trevor most strongly emphasized the need for a more prolonged and systematic process of training and education in Japanese methods for British personnel of Japanese firms operating in Great Britain, and this need is equally evident in the Canadian scene. The success in this area of activity by Japanese firms operating in Canada may in fact determine a new type of "branch plant," differentiated from many other foreign-owned firms, preceding them both in structure and function.

JME's head office must finally come to realize that it will be a number of years before Canadians can be delegated the full responsibility of running the operation of its Simcoe Bay plant. Whether or not the plant will ever become self-sufficient in the sense that Canadian staff and managers take over the full responsibility for running it is still open to question. It seems rather unlikely at this moment. The issue of localization, however valid and feasible it may be seen from Tokyo, looks far from being settled in the near future in Simcoe Bay.

The question often raised in the course of this data analysis was how else could JME have proceeded. Even with the constraints it was compelled to accomodate, were there any other options that the company could have but failed to explore? While agreeing to work with a labour organization and accepting the existing union as an agent, the company still could have negotiated a new contract on its own terms instead of taking over the existing one. According to the labour laws in the province, a new owner taking over a business enterprise is obliged to take over and work with the existing union – the succession rights of union – but not necessarily to take over the existing labour contract. Upon taking over the business from Arcan JME did not enter into a vigorous negotiation to produce a new contract, something which seemed almost a mystery to outsiders. As a matter of fact, we were told by an informant that the first contract, however tentative, was struck in two days without any substantial negotiations or even discussions about specific issues.[2] No advice from consulting lawyers and government agencies seems to have been forthcoming in this matter, and its importance was overlooked by the newly appointed management.

Our general impression is that Japanese firms in general, including JME, clearly lack the familiarity required to engage effectively in designing the structure of relations with their employees and union, and the knowledge required to work with the union to renegotiate the contract, including succession rights of the union. Also, the Japanese management at JME seemed largely unfamiliar with factory working practices in the Canadian plant. After it negotiated a second contract with the union in which the first substantial bargaining took place, the Japanese management gradually became more acquainted with the basic principles regulating the industrial relations of this country and formal negotiating arrangements. Still, it will need "years' [of] learning and experience," according to an executive member of the union, to get a full understanding of the mechanisms of collective bargaining and other critical aspects of Canadian labour-management relations. Labour-management relations are still strained occasionally as the union seeks to protect its members against changes in practices which appear to be arbitrary and poorly designed.

A Canadian study (Godard and Kochan, 1982) identifies nineteen issues to be bargained for in a labour-management contract negotiation, and assesses empirically the relative importance of each of the issues. Such issues as compensation, job security and management rights, procedural issues including seniority provisions and workplace rules and disciplines, and union-security and rights issues are noted as issues most vigorously bargained for in contract negotiations in Canada. Collective bargaining involves a series of trade-offs between the preferences of management and those of the union. To be an effective bargainer, some knowledge of Canadian industrial relations at the present time is essential. Yet, that knowledge and understanding are impossible to obtain without some knowledge of the origins and development of the institution itself. Therefore, Japanese firms seem to have a fair amount of homework to do in order to become educated and experienced in this area regardless of the type of union with which they might be dealing.

Similarly, it is impossible to understand the Simcoe Bay plant as it was without some knowledge and background on the way the manufacturing industry has traditionally operated in Canada. The fact that the industry has largely been controlled by foreign-owned companies, and that the Simcoe Bay plant was one of the many American-owned branch plants operating in this country, has had significant implications for the understanding of the way that the plant was run and why it had to be shut down. Because it lacked a basic understanding of the way a branch plant operates and of "branch plant mentality" in general, JME did not realize until some time after it took over the plant that the Simcoe Bay operation had done little design work in its twenty years of operation and that it had never really built up a solid engineering base. It was only then that JME began to understand the consequences of the legacy of American investment and American organizational design in Canada.

Because of this outside ownership and control, Canadian manufacturing has a weak industrial base which extends to its supply base as well. JME originally assumed that there were "enough suppliers out there," and gave a high priority to establishing "close and lasting" business relationships with local suppliers. However, it soon encountered "many obstacles" in its attempt to explore the potential suppliers both of materials and of engineering services, obstacles which are still far from being resolved satisfactorily. The supply base consisting of local suppliers is fragmented and "too small," so that no element of selection exists at all; many crucial parts and materials are almost impossible to obtain in the area or even in the neighbouring metropolitan area, not the ones of quality at least. This supply base, which is far weaker and has fewer supporting services than the Japanese firm anticipated, has much to do with foreign investment and control of the industry, another constraint that JME has had to accommodate. While Japanese manufacturers prefer to build up an exclusive relationship with long-run suppliers, the JME management has just begun making contact with some suppliers, and it will be a long time before it can establish a satisfactory business relationship with them.

The takeover process from the former owner to the new, it must be noted, took place not only in a hurry but in a highly political fashion, as is often the case in this country. The Simcoe Bay plant had been closed for six months, and the nine hundred employees were out of jobs when JME made the decision to purchase it. Under these circumstances, the pressure on JME to act quickly and to speed up its decision-making process was enormous. Governments, both federal and provincial, together with the politicians representing the Simcoe Bay area, were actively involved in looking for a potential buyer for the closed plant, and in the process of negotiating they exercised a fair amount of power and pressure to pursuade JME to purchase the plant and to reopen the business as soon as possible. Welcoming a new owner to the area is one thing, but giving the newly arriving firm meaningful preparation to ensure its smooth operation is another matter. "They [the governments] know how to provide incentives to invite firms to invest in the province, but they don't know how to care for them after they come," was one of the comments heard during our field work. There is no guarantee that the rescued business will become a viable business enterprise for its new owner, particularly when the new owner happens to be coming from the other side of the world with new technology and with very different management techniques than the existing ones.

Obviously, whether or not such a rescued business becomes successful should be of prime importance to the various levels of government, particularly in light of the amount of taxpayers' money invested in the transformation of the business. Programs for giving "after-care" should therefore be given high priority by the concerned government. We believe that this applies to other foreign firms, not only to Japanese ones.

No doubt government offers of low interest loans and grants are attractive to firms considering investment, but these firms should be aware that the money obliges them to follow the directions given by the governments. In return for the subsidies they receive, these firms are required to make promises and to fulfill them. JME made several promises which have considerably restricted their ability to implement change. One of them was made during the initial contract signed after "the two days' negotiation" between JME and the union, and it provided that the company would use Arcan's seniority list for recall purposes. Recalling the laid-off workers and providing them with jobs in the midst of the recession was a part of the deal between the government and JME. Whether or not it was a good deal for JME, it forced the company to start up the operation almost at once so that the laid off ex-Arcan workers could regain their jobs. Under these conditions JME was forced to accept the business enterprise in its totality including terms of conditions which would later prove unsatisfactory.

JME's investment in the Simcoe Bay plant was the first substantial attempt by a Japanese firm to become involved in manufacturing activities in Canada. Following JME's lead several Japanese firms soon announced major investment plans, mostly in the automobile sector. The first Japanese company which started assembling cars in Canada three years ago opted to adopt a completely no-constraint approach, following the policy set by the head office of the firm. It is instructive to compare this company's experience to that of JME's. This particular auto manufacturer did not seek government grants when it announced that it would invest in Canada, and declared that it would pursue its non-union policy. The company has so far been fairly successful in terms of production performance and of the quality of cars it has produced. The president of this company, in an article recently published in a leading Canadian newspaper,[3] described his company and emphasized the importance of transferring to its Canadian plant the techniques of problem solving developed by the parent company, including techniques of thinking, working and communicating with employees. He also stressed that building everything from scratch has been essential to the company's success in Canada.

This auto-maker started its operation by recruiting a relatively small number of workers from the rural and largely agrarian local labour market in which it is located, and added more workers as its plant grew. Most of the recruited are young workers with a high school education. Some of them have had manufacturing experience, but virtually none had experience in automobile manufacturing. This applies to the managerial staff as well. The entire work force thus consists of "amateurs" in car-making, according to the president. Starting with a work force consisting only of inexperienced employees has not been easy, and training this work force has turned out to be a costly venture for the company. Over one hundred expatriate technicians were sent over from Japan to give on-the-job training for the first year of the operation. A large number of Canadian personnel has also been sent either to its home plant in Japan or to its U.S. subsidiary for a specially designed training purpose. The company keeps sending technicians and trainers from Japan whenever it is considered necessary and appropriate to do so. Employees are expected through direct and intense interaction with expatriates to thoroughly understand that the basic concept underlying their production activities is a team rather than an individual definition of responsibility and of decision-making.

Two other Japanese auto manufacturers will start manufacturing cars in Canada in the near future. Both seem to be adopting a more constrained approach than did the company cited above. They have accepted grants from the federal government. One of them is a joint venture with the largest auto-maker in North America. It negotiated with the national labour union before it made a decision to invest in Canada (with the anticipation that its plant will be unionized). According to reports in the media, the major items for negotiation were simplified job classifications, flexible work rules, and other innovations. The country's strongest industrial union was prepared to be more innovative in the type of contracts and work rules; the negotiations turned out to be a fruitful process.

This successful negotiation with the union signals that in fact constraints can work for Japanese firms if they are handled sensitively. All Japanese companies deciding to invest, including the three cited above as well as other small ones, are aware that they will need to manage their human resources carefully in order to succeed. They place strong emphasis on recruitment, and are expending enormous efforts to select the desired type of work force. It is true that by hiring new employees, they do not have to deal with the problems JME inherited when it agreed to rehire ex-Arcan employees. However, JME's problems in dealing with its employees stemmed in large measure from its inexperience in dealing with North American workers in general, and the solutions it adopted and failed to adopt, as outlined in the present study, can be a very useful guide for all Japanese firms planning to establish a presence in Canada.

Japanese firms thinking of setting up plants in Canada have a number of alternatives to consider, and would be wise to weigh them carefully before making a decision about which to adopt. While choosing an unconstrained approach to management by establishing a plant from scratch, as most of the firms so far in North America have done, appears to be the easiest option, it may not necessarily be the fastest, nor always the most desirable. By studying and learning from the experience of JME at its Simcoe Bay plant, Japanese firms interested in the Canadian market may find that accepting the limitations imposed by an existing plant, an existing union, and the restrictions imposed by government grants may in fact be desirable if undertaken deliberately, with great care and with awareness of all the possible pitfalls.

Notes

1. Every organization operates under constraints. It is constrained by the interests of others – governments, consumers, unions, competitors, etc. (Pfeffer and Salancik, 1978: 14-16). It appeared that JME chose to accept the existing constraints, as they were aware of them, rather than to reduce them. In reality, however, it may be more accurate to state that it was forced to do so. The action of the organization can thus be better interpreted within the context of adjustment that JME had gone through to conform to the constraints imposed by the particular social context under which it operated.

2. This rather quick start-up is in sharp contrast with the approach adopted by Toyota in establishing its first auto manufacturing plant in North America. It was a joint venture with GM. The two companies, operating under the name New United Motor Manufacturing Inc., refurbished a closed GM plant in Fremont, California and began production in 1984. Like JME, Toyota took over the previously unionized plant and went through the whole process of reorganizing it. According to documents (Rehder, et al., 1985), Toyota's process of reorgainzing the American plant was deliberately slow. They took one full year in negotiating with GM to materialize the joint venture to begin with. With the existing union, UAW, the new company had six months to produce a 17-page letter of intent, and only after the exchange of the letter, did they decide to recognize the union as a bargaining agent. The first formal collective bargaining agreement between the new company and the union was signed after "tough bargaining" almost two years after the two sides met for the first time.

3. The Toronto Star, March 3, 1988.

APPENDIX I

THE JME PLANT

Questionnaire/Interview Schedule for Workers

This is a study about how your see your job, what you like and dislike about it. The study is funded by the federal government. The purpose of the survey is to learn how you feel about different aspects of your work, your supervisors, the companies for which you have worked. The results will be kept confidential. No one will be able to tell you how you answered the questions. The results will be reported for all people in this plant. Some will be compared to those working in plants in Great Britain.

Please do not write your name anywhere on the questionnaire.

Your cooperation is very much appreciated.

PLEASE CIRCLE (OR CHECK LIKE ✔) THE APPROPRIATE RESPONSE OR FILL IN THE BLANKS.

The first section deals with your current and previous jobs. Some of the questions compare JME and Arcan. *If you didn't work for Arcan, answer such questions NA (not applicable).*

1. In your view, what are the most important differences between the way work was done at Arcan and the way it is done at JME?

    _____

    _____

    _____

2. Which Arcan practices should JME adopt?

    _____

    _____

    _____

3. Which aspects of work at JME do you prefer?

    _____

    _____

    _____

4. Are shift meetings introduced by JME
    _____very useful?
    _____Somewhat useful?
    _____not at all useful?
    _____we don't have shift meetings
    _____don't know

5. Are monthly meetings introduced by JME
    _____very useful?
    _____somewhat useful?
    _____not at all useful?
    _____don't know

6. Do you feel that job rotation (check all that apply)

    _____makes work more interesting?

    _____reduces my ability to do the job right?

    _____leaves me unsure of what to expect?

    _____increases my workload?

    _____haven't been involved in job rotation

    _____other. Please specify_____

    _____don't know

7. Do you prefer the Arcan or JME approach to quality control and quality assurance?

    _____prefer JME approach

    _____prefer the Arcan approach

    _____both are inadequate

    _____NA (didn't work for Arcan)

    _____don't know

8. Are the following features of employment of JME above or below average?

	Above average	Average	Below average		
	1	2	3	4	5
a. type of management	1	2	3	4	5
b. nature of the work	1	2	3	4	5
c. job security	1	2	3	4	5
d. money you can earn	1	2	3	4	5
e. hours of shifts	1	2	3	4	5
f. working conditions	1	2	3	4	5
g. chance of getting a better job	1	2	3	4	5
h. opportunity to learn or use skill	1	2	3	4	5

9. Does JME consider the following to be very important, somewhat important or not at all important?

	Very important		Somewhat important		Not at all important
	1	2	3	4	5

		Very important	Somewhat important	Not at all important		
a.	good relations between workers and management	1	2	3	4	5
b.	managers showing appreciation to workers who cope well with problems	1	2	3	4	5
c.	concern for a friendly atmosphere	1	2	3	4	5
d.	company trust in employees	1	2	3	4	5
e.	providing help with personal problems	1	2	3	4	5
f.	willingness to train me	1	2	3	4	5
g.	interest shown in my point of view	1	2	3	4	5

10. Did Arcan consider the following to be very important, somewhat important or not at all important?

	Very important		Somewhat important		Not at all important
	1	2	3	4	5

		Very important	Somewhat important	Not at all important		
a.	good relations between workers and management	1	2	3	4	5
b.	managers showing appreciation to workers who cope well with problems	1	2	3	4	5
c.	concern for a friendly atmosphere	1	2	3	4	5
d.	company trust in employees	1	2	3	4	5
e.	providing help with personal problems	1	2	3	4	5
f.	willingness to train me	1	2	3	4	5
g.	interest shown in my point of view	1	2	3	4	5

11. How much emphasis does JME place on the following practices within the plant?

		Very important		Somewhat important		Not at all important
		1	2	3	4	5

a.	thoroughness of planning	1	2	3	4	5
b.	efficiency with which work is organized	1	2	3	4	5
c.	concern with quality of work	1	2	3	4	5
d.	concern with quality of service	1	2	3	4	5
e.	amount of checking & double checking	1	2	3	4	5
f.	own time spent on checking	1	2	3	4	5
g.	work checked by others	1	2	3	4	5
h.	emphasis on rules & procedures	1	2	3	4	5
i.	strictness about mistakes	1	2	3	4	5
j.	strictness about discipline & time keeping	1	2	3	4	5
k.	management interest in the details or work	1	2	3	4	5

12. How much emphasis did Arcan place on the following practices within the plant?

		Very important		Somewhat important		Not at all important
		1	2	3	4	5

a.	thoroughness of planning	1	2	3	4	5
b.	efficiency with which work is organized	1	2	3	4	5
c.	concern with quality of work	1	2	3	4	5
d.	concern with quality of service	1	2	3	4	5

e.	amount of checking & double checking	1	2	3	4	5
f.	own time spent on checking	1	2	3	4	5
g.	work checked by others	1	2	3	4	5
h.	emphasis on rules & procedures	1	2	3	4	5
i.	strictness about mistakes	1	2	3	4	5
j.	strictness about discipline & time keeping	1	2	3	4	5
k.	management interest in the details or work	1	2	3	4	5

13. How well informed are you about what happens at JME? Are you

_____very well informed?

_____fairly well informed?

_____not well informed?

_____don't know

14. How well informed were you about what happened at Arcan? Were you

_____very well informed?

_____fairly well informed?

_____not well informed?

_____don't know

_____didn't work for Arcan

15. How much influence do the following groups of people have on what happens in this JME plant?

	Great influence		Some influence		No influence
	1	2	3	4	5

a.	plant manager	1	2	3	4	5
b.	other managers & supervisors	1	2	3	4	5
c.	workers as a group	1	2	3	4	5
d.	employee (union) representatives	1	2	3	4	5
e.	you personally	1	2	3	4	5

174

16. How much influence did the following groups of people have on what happened in the Arcan plant?

	Great influence		Some influence		No influence
	1	2	3	4	5

		Great influence	Some influence		No influence
a.	plant manager	1	2	3	4	5
b.	other managers & supervisors	1	2	3	4	5
c.	workers as a group	1	2	3	4	5
d.	employee (union) representatives	1	2	3	4	5
e.	you personally	1	2	3	4	5

17. To what extent do you feel responsible for the success of:

	Very much		Somewhat		Not at all
	1	2	3	4	5

a.	your own work group	1	2	3	4	5
b.	your department	1	2	3	4	5
c.	the whole plant	1	2	3	4	5

18. Please name your supervisor:_____

19. My SUPERVISOR is:

	Very likely			Somewhat likely			Unlikely	
	1	2	3	4	5	6	7

a.	to help subordinates with personal problems	1	2	3	4	5	6	7

b.   to encourage participation in
important decisions   1   2   3   4   5   6   7

c.   to be fair with sub-
ordinates   1   2   3   4   5   6   7

d.   to demand people give their best
effort all the time   1   2   3   4   5   6   7

e.   to leave it up to me to decide how to
go about my job   1   2   3   4   5   6   7

f.   to defend subordinates to
"higher ups"   1   2   3   4   5   6   7

g.   to treat each subordinate as an
important individual 1   2   3   4   5   6   7

h.   to evaluate my performance
accurately   1   2   3   4   5   6   7

i.   to be trustworthy   1   2   3   4   5   6   7

j.   to be concerned about me as a
person   1   2   3   4   5   6   7

k.   to behave competently 1   2   3   4   5   6   7

20.   For what employers other than Arcan and JME have you worked? Please start with the first full-time job you held.

First Job

a.   What was the first firm you worked for?_____

b.   Whereabout was that?_____

c.   How long did you work there?_____

d.   Why did you leave?_____

e.   What were the main tasks you performed there?_____

Second Job

a.   _____

b.   _____

c.   _____

d.   _____

e.   _____

Third Job

a._____

b._____

c._____

d._____

e._____

Other Job

a._____

b._____

c._____

d._____

e._____

21.   Casting your mind back over all the jobs you have ever held including your present job, which have you liked the best? Why?_____

_____

_____

_____

22.   Is your current job a good job? Using the following scale, how satisfied are you with various aspects of your present job?

Very satisfied		Somewhat satisfied		Very unsatisfied	
1	2	3	4	5	6

a. how you get on with management

1	2	3	4	5	6

b. the security of the job   1   2   3   4   5   6

c. how worthwhile the job is   1   2   3   4   5   6

d. the interest, skill & effort required   1   2   3   4   5   6

e. fringe benefits like the pension, sick pay or social facilities   1   2   3   4   5   6

f. training   1   2   3   4   5   6

g. trade union strength   1   2   3   4   5   6

h.	friendliness of the people with whom you work	1	2	3	4	5	6
i.	hours of work, including traveling time	1	2	3	4	5	6
j.	opportunity to do your work in your own way	1	2	3	4	5	6
k.	working conditions	1	2	3	4	5	6
l.	chances for promotion	1	2	3	4	5	6
m.	pay	1	2	3	4	5	6

23. Are you thinking of changing jobs in the near future?

_____Yes

_____weighing the possibility

_____No

_____don't know

24. If Yes or weighing the possibility, why are you thinking of leaving your job?_____

_____

_____

25. How much more per week would you have to be paid in order to change jobs?

_____would move if paid what I earn now

_____$10 more per week

_____$20 more per week

_____$30 more per week

_____$40 more per week

_____$50 more per week

_____don't know

26. If you had two job offers and you were trying to decide between them, how important would the following factors be in making your decision?

		Important			Somewhat important		Very important			
		1	2	3	4	5	6			
a.	how you get on with management				1	2	3	4	5	6
b.	the security of the job				1	2	3	4	5	6
c.	how worthwhile the job is				1	2	3	4	5	6
d.	the interest, skill & effort required				1	2	3	4	5	6
e.	fringe benefits like the pension, sick pay or social facilities				1	2	3	4	5	6
f.	continuous training				1	2	3	4	5	6
g.	trade union strength				1	2	3	4	5	6
h.	friendliness of the people with whom you work				1	2	3	4	5	6
i.	hours of work, including time spent traveling				1	2	3	4	5	6
j.	opportunity to do your work in your own way				1	2	3	4	5	6
k.	working conditions				1	2	3	4	5	6
l.	opportunity for promotion				1	2	3	4	5	6
m.	pay				1	2	3	4	5	6

27. In your experience, what do you think is the best way to get ahead? Is it to stay with the same firm for a long time or is it to move around between them?

_____stay with JME

_____move from one firm to another

_____don't know

28. How likely is it that JME will lay-off workers in the future leaving you temporarily unemployed?

_____very unlikely

_____somewhat likely

_____very likely

_____don't know

29. How likely is it that JME will fire long-term employees leaving you unemployed?
     _____very unlikely
     _____somewhat likely
     _____very likely

30. Five years from now, what would you like your job to be, if things went really well for you?
     Same firm?   ___Yes
                         ___No
     Same line of work? ___Yes
                         ___No
     Job title?_____

31. If you could start your working life over again, would you choose this kind of job?
     _____Yes
     _____No
     _____don't know

32. Do you feel that your work is worthwhile, a valuable part of your life, or is it just something you do to earn a living?
     _____work is worthwhile
     _____not sure
     _____work only to earn a living
     _____don't know

33. Did you find the time you spent at work with Arcan more or less interesting than your present work?
     _____working for Arcan was more interesting
     _____no difference
     _____working for JME is more interesting
     _____didn't work for Arcan
     _____don't know

34. Since JME has fewer employees than Arcan
    a. has your influence increased? _____Yes_____No
    b. has your responsibility increased? _____Yes_____No
    c. has your workload increased? _____Yes_____No
    d. is it easier to get things done? _____Yes_____No
    e. has your job become more stressful? _____Yes_____No

35. When you start off for work, how often, if at all, do you find yourself thinking: "I don't want to go in today."
    _____often
    _____sometimes
    _____rarely
    _____never

Lastly, we would like you to provide some background details.

37. Are you ____male or ____female?

38. When did you start working at JME? _____   19____
    　　　　　　　　　　　　　　　　　　　　　month　　　year

39. What is your normal job at JME?
    _____

40. Is there any other job at JME you would rather do?
    _____Yes
    _____No
    _____don't know
    　　　If Yes, which one? _____

41. Was your normal job at Arcan the same one you have now?
    _____Yes
    _____No
    _____didn't work for Arcan
    　　　If No: Do you have _____more responsibility now?
    　　　　　　　　　　　　　_____about the same responsibility?
    　　　　　　　　　　　　　_____less responsibility now?
    　　　　　　　　　　　　　_____don't know

42. When did you start working at Arcan _____   19____
           month   year
           _____ didn't work for Arcan

43. How many times did you change jobs at Arcan?_____
           _____ didn't work for Arcan

44. When were you laid off from Arcan _____   19____
           month   year

45. Did you take another job while you were waiting to be recalled?
 _____No
 _____Yes for_____as a
      Name of company

  _____
     Job title

46. With the exception of the period when Arcan was closed, have you ever been unemployed for longer than a few days?
 _____No
 _____Yes for_____months

47. In what year were you born? 19____

48. Where were you born? _____
    If born outside Canada, when did you immigrate? 19__

49. Where did you live during most of your childhood?

 _____

50. How old where you when you left full-time education?_____

51. Please indicate the last school you attended on a full-time basis:

	In Canada	Abroad
University	_____	_____
Community college	_____	_____
Collegiate	_____	_____
Technical vocational high school	_____	_____
Commercial high school	_____	_____
Junior high school	_____	_____
Elementary school	_____	_____

52. What was the last grade you completed?_____

53. While at school or since, have you acquired any formal qualifications?

    _____Yes

    _____No

    If Yes: Please list_____

    _____

54. What was your father's job at the time you left school?

    _____

55. What is your marital status?

    _____never married

    _____married

    _____separated, divorced or widowed

    If married: Is your spouse:

    _____employed part-time? Earns $_____yearly

    _____employed full-time? Earns $_____yearly

    _____at home

    _____unemployed

56. How many children do you have? _____

    How many live at home_____

    Are any of those at home working? If Yes, how many?_____

57. How long on average does it take you to get to work?_____

                                                          minutes

58. For the past week how many hours did you work?

    _____regular hours

    _____overtime hours

59. Do you:

    _____rent your home?

    _____own your home?

    _____live with someone who pays the rent/mortgage?

60. Are you currently or have you ever held an office in a union?

_____Yes

_____No

61. When you retire what would you hope to do?

_____

_____

THANK YOU FOR YOUR ASSISTANCE.

Now that you have completed the questionnaire, fill in the blue card and deposit it in the card box. We will make an appointment to interview you.

APPENDIX II

Letter from the Researchers

May, 1986

Dear JME Employees,

This study is the first in Canada to assess the reaction of Canadian workers to Japanese management as practiced in Canada. The questionnaire we are asking you to complete is long but we ask you to complete all questions. Some may seem repetitious, but they are needed to compare Canadian with British workers.

Your responses will be confidential. No-one will know how you answered the questions as long as you return the questionnaire sealed in the envelope provided. *We ask you to return the blue card separately.* Place it in the box labelled blue cards, so that we can send reminders to those who have not returned their questionnaires. If we are to accurately reflect your views, we must have a 100% return rate. Please help us to achieve that rate.

One-third of you will be asked to spend half an hour being interviewed in addition to completing the questionnaire so that we can get a fuller understanding of employee views. We have randomly selected those to be interviewed from a list of employees.

The result of this study will be shared with you and we will suggest ways based on your responses of improving the working environment in this plant.

Please return your questionnaire to the questionnaire box located in the cafeteria no later than May 30. Thank you.

Signed

Letter from the President of Local Union

May 1986

To All Members C.W.C. Local 532

Dear Brother/Sister,

The questionnaire included here is part of a study being done on the workers' feelings on Japanese ownership compared to North American ownership. This study is being compared with similar studies done in England. The study is funded by The Federal government and is in no way connected with a manufacturer past or present.

The questionnaire is completely anonymous and can be deposited in the box provided in the cafeteria. Although some of the questions may seem off-base, it is a general worker attitude they are looking for.

I urge you to participate in this study and to be honest with your answers. Consider this an opportunity to state your true feelings and views. If you have any doubts or concerns, please feel free to contact me.

In solidarity,

Signed
President
CWC Local 532

References

Abegglen, James C. and Stalk, George, Jr.
1985   *KAISHA, The Japanese Corporation. New York: Basic Books Inc.*

Becker, Howard
1970   *Sociological Work.* Chicago: Aldine Publishing Co.

Bourgault, Pierre L.
1972   *Innovation and the Structure of Canadian Industry.* Background Study for the Science Council of Canada. Ottawa: Information Canada.

Burns, T. and Stalker, G. M.
1961   *The Management of Innovation.* London: Tavistock.

Burnstein M., Tienhaara, N., Hewson, P. and Warrander, P. B.
1975   *Canadian Work Values: Findings of a Work Ethic Survey and Job Satisfaction Survey.* Ottawa: Information Canada.

Clark, Rodney
1979   *The Japanese Company.* New Haven: Yale University Press.

Cole, Robert E.
1979   *Work, Mobility, and Participation.* Berkeley, California: University of California Press.

1971   *Japanese Blue Collar.* Berkeley, California: University of California Press.

Cusumano, Michael A.
1985   *The Japanese Automobile Industry.* Cambridge, Mass.: The Harvard University Press.

Daft, Richard L.
1983   *Organization Theory and Design.* St. Paul, Minnesota: West Publishing Co.

Doeringer, Peter B. and Piore, Michael J.
1971   *Internal Labor Markets and Manpower Analysis.* Lexington, Mass.: O.C. Heath and Company.

Dore, Ronald
1973   *British Factory-Japanese Factory.* Berkeley, California: University of California Press.

1982   "Introduction" in Kamata, Satoshi, *Japan in the Passing Lane.* New York: Pantheon Books, pp. ix-x.

English, H.E.
1971   "Foreign Ownership Reviewed:" *Canadian Economic Issues:*
            Pal, I.D. (ed.). Toronto: Macmillan of Canada, pp. 549-562.

Gardner, B. B. and Whyte, W. F.
1945   "The Man in the Middle: Position and Problems of the
            Foreman," *Applied Anthropology (Human Organization)* 2, 4:
            pp. 1-28.

Godard, John H. and Kochan, Thomas A.
1982   "Canadian Management under Collective Bargaining: Policies,
            Process, Structure, and Effectiveness," in Anderson, John and
            Gunderson, Morley (eds.), *Union-Management Relations in
            Canada.* Don Mills, Ontario: Addison-Wesley Canada.

Goldthorpe, J. H.
1959   "Technical Organization as a Factor in Supervisor/Worker
            Conflict." *British Journal of Sociology.* Vol. 10, pp. 213-230.

Goldthorpe, J. H., Lockwood, David, Bechhofer, Frank and Platt, Jennifer.
1960   *The Affluent Worker: Industrial Attitudes and Behaviour.*
            Cambridge: Cambridge University Press.

Government of Canada
1972   *Foreign Direct Investment in Canada.* Ottawa: Information
            Canada.

Grayson, Paul
1985   *Corporate Strategy and Plant Closures: The SFK Experience.*
            Toronto: Our Times Publishing.

Grimm, James W. and Dunn, Thomas P.
1986   "The Contemporary Foreman Status". *Work and Occupations.*
            Vol. 13, No.3, pp. 359-376.

Grinker, William, Cooke, Donald and Kirsch, Arther
1970   *Climbing the Job Ladder.* Washington, D.C.: National Institute
            of Education, U.S. Office of Health, Education, and Welfare
            (reprint).

Gust, G. M.
1971   "Discovering Management's Forgotten Man - the Foreman."
            Personnel Administration. September-October: pp. 34-36.

Koike, Kazuo
1984   "Skill Formation Systems in the U.S. and Japan: A
            Comparative Study" in Aoki, Masahiko (ed.) *The Economic
            Analysis of the Japanese Firm.* Amsterdam: North-Holland.
            pp.47-75.

Makabe, Tomoko
1984   *The Japanese-Owned and Managed Businesses in Canada.*
            Working Paper #28. Toronto: Toronto-York Joint Centre on
            Modern East Asia, York University.

Mintzberg, Henry
1979   *The Structuring of Organization.* Englewood Cliff, N.J.:
            Prentice-Hall.

Monden, Yasuhiro.
1985   "Japanese Production Management." in Monden, Y. et al.
            (eds.), *Innovations in Management: The Japanese Corporation.*
            Atlanta, Georgia: Industrial Engineering and Management
            Press, pp. 73-85.

1983   *Toyota Production System.* Atlanta, Georgia: Industrial
            Engineering and Management Press.

Nightingale, Donald V.
1983   *Workplace Democracy.* Toronto: University of Toronto Press.

Ontario Select Committee on Economic and Cultural Nationalism.
1974   *Foreign Ownership: Corporate Behaviour and Public Attitudes,*
            Overview Report.

Paterson, T. T.
1966   *Management Theory.* London: Business Publications
            Ltd.

Pfeffer, Jeffrey and Salanacik, Gerald R.
1978   *The External Control of Organization.* New York: Harper &
            Row, Publishers.

Pugh, S. S., Hickson, D. J., Hinings, C. R. and Turner, C.
1968   "Dimensions of Organization Structure. *Administrative Science
            Quarterly:* pp. 65-105.

Quinn, Robert P. and Shepard, Linda J.
1974   *The 1972-73 Quality of Employment Survey.* Ann Arbor,
            Michigan: Survey Research Center, University of Michigan.

Rehder, Robert R., Hendry, Robert W. and Smith, Marta M.
1985   "NUMMI: The Best of Both Worlds?," *Management Review,*
            December: pp. 36-41.

Safarian, A.E.
1966   *Foreign Ownership of Canadian Industry.* Toronto: McGraw-
                Hill Co. of Canada.

Schonberger, Richard J.
1982   *Japanese Manufacturing Techniques.* New York: The Free
                Press.

Shimada, Haruo and MacDuffie, John Paul
1987   "Industrial Relations and 'Humanware': An Analysis of
                Japanese Investment in Automobile Manufacturing Industry in
                the United States," A Briefing Paper for the First Policy
                Forum, International Motor Vehicles Program, May 4, 1987.

Slichter, Sumner H., Healy, James J. and Livernash, E. Robert
1960   *The Impact of Collective Bargaining on Management.*
                Washington, D.C.: The Brookings Institution.

Takamiya, Makoto
1981   "Japanese Multinationals in Europe: Internal Operations and
                their Public Policy Implications." *Columbia Journal of World
                Business* 16: pp. 5-17.

Thompson, James D.
1967   *Organizations in Action.* New York: McGraw-Hill Book
                Company.

Walker, C. R. and Guest, R. H.
1952   *The Man on the Assembly Line.* Cambridge, Mass: Harvard
                University Press.

Warr, Peter B. and Wall, Toby
1975   *Work and Well- Being.* London: Penguin Books.

Watkins, M. H.
1968   *Foreign Ownership and the Structure of Canadian Industry.*
                Ottawa: Privy Council.

White, Michael and Trevor, Malcolm.
1983   *Under Japanese Management: The Experience of British Workers.*
                London: Heinemann.

Woodward, Joan
1965   *Industrial Organization: Theory and Practice.* Oxford: Oxford
                University Press.

Wray, D. F.
1949   "Marginal Man of Industry, the Foreman," *American Journal of
                Sociology.* 54: pp. 298-301.

Wright, Richard M.
1983   "The Elusive Alliance: Japanese Business in Canada."
              Discussion Paper. Montreal: McGill University.

Yoshino, M. Y.
1976   *Japan's Multinational Enterprises*. Cambridge,
              Massachusetts: Harvard University Press.

INDEX